Jakeb Brasee's

THE ART & SCIENCE OF FINISHING LAST

how to bless your sisters' hearts and get away with it

Skyfort Publishing

1st Edition, June 2009

Copyright © 2009 by Jakeb Brasee

Book cover, design, and illustrations also by Jakeb Brasee, in fact.

Bible verses are quoted from the ESV, NASB, NIV, NKJV, and NLT.

Published by Skyfort Publishing
P.O. Box 21, Oberlin OH 44074

ISBN 978-0-9824953-0-8

Printed in the United States of America

For Bethany and Chisomo

"Treat younger women with all purity as you would

your own sisters."

-- 1 Timothy 5:2

Table o' Lessons

Table o' Missions

A PREFACE

Like all of my endeavors, this book is a product of the epic battle that rages in the upset stomach of my soul. I am a man sorely divided between the two Great Desires, which are "Being Nice to Girls" and "Being a Ninja".

Thankfully, this torturous rift is made less excruciating by the hopeful fact that the Great Desires are not mutually exclusive, nor even especially standoffish.

Emboldened by this knowledge I began a journey through the bewildering halls of my battered psyche and the great broad baffling expanses of the world. I set out looking for that most elusive of creatures -- my self. I sought to unify the shards of my identity, to become a whole person, balanced, assured, well-adjusted.

Failing that, I tripped down the dark path of the Shadow Gentleman, and there I found my place.

Who dares trip with me for a while? Do you? You can have this cool badge:

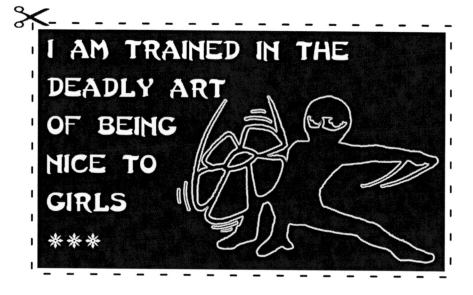

Three things to note before proceeding:

1. My journey down the Shadow Gentleman's road is a part of my lifelong attempt to follow the way of my master and teacher and Lord, Mr. Jesus Christ. Unless you have followed Him into the family of God, much of my talk about brotherly love will not make perfect sense. It is fair to mention it straightaway. You can still glean something useful from these pages without following Him, but nothing useful enough to save your life.

2. This book is divided into lessons and missions which reflect the road I have walked (or often failed to walk). The missions are not just for reading, but for doing -- and not just for doing once, but as a lifelong practice. Shadow Gentlemen are not mere theoreticians!

3. I have tried to avoid undue repetition. Undue repetition is unduly repetitive. Therefore I have tried to avoid it. What I mean is, I have tried not to repeat things unless they seriously deserve repeating. Otherwise, no repeating. Be aware, then, that little ideas are pivots for big ones.

Your training begins when you turn the page. Turn it slowly. Relish the moment.

ORIENTATION -- LESSON 1. YOU

*"In a game of rock, paper, scissors
introspection loses to all three."
-- Pearson Threepieces
  (in one of his more lucid moments)*

The motto of the Shadow Gentleman is...well, the motto is actually an interval of comfortable silence. But one of the first rules is this: *you are not the point.* This book is not for you. You will get nothing out of it, at least not on purpose. You must not be in it for yourself, or you will do no good; at very best, you will merely do no evil. So what are you, then? You are a means to an end. You will care for the girls in your sphere of influence. Their best interests are your interest. Your own edification concerns me only so far as it benefits your sisters. Not that you are worth nothing, but you must set yourself aside and attend to them, because they need you.

Your mysterious inclinations, your subtlety and precision and repressed desire to run on walls -- these things can be harnessed and used. We will talk more of that in a little while. But you do not begin by learning how to strike! You must first learn how to learn. Your greatest weapons are your eyes and your ears and your mind. You cannot be invisible until you have learned to see. You cannot be silent until you have learned to listen. You cannot defeat what you do not know. You get the idea.

For that reason, we begin with a consideration of our sisters and their needs.

ORIENTATION -- LESSON 2. HER

"Just your sister? Just! Sooner say torture tickles, no one is ever 'just'!"
-- Peytr Almonet

The astute reader will notice that I have been referring to the ladies in question as our "sisters". There is a reason for this; in the Bible, young pastor Timothy is instructed to treat young women "as sisters, in all purity." (1 Timothy 5:2) It seems like very good advice to me, so I recommend it to all men in their friendships with women, not just to pastors in their ministry. There may be a better idea, but has anyone ever thought of it? Is there any alternative relationship that is safer, more encouraging, more honorable, more permanently good? I cannot think of one, so I will continue to speak of your Christian female friends as your sisters.

Along these same lines, it has been my experience that girls have a great need for good brothers. A young woman is beset on all sides by powerful and discouraging forces. Every day, the world challenges her to prove her worth -- acceptance based on performance or appearance. Criticism comes quickly, while approval comes grudgingly and with ulterior motives. From within, she is assaulted by emotions, fears, yearnings, and sins. Satan's legions (if you will take the spiritual battlefield seriously) are eager to trap her or destroy her. And always she must beware of evil men. These are the *minimal* trials of her life. She cannot expect it to get much better than this, and she can expect it to get much worse (through specific difficulties, like illness or an unloving family or any string of peculiar hardships).

It is easy for her to doubt her value. It is also easy for her to feel alone, threatened, or hopeless. It is easy to be confused. Now, women are not helpless or friendless, and God's mercies are new every morning. I am not trying to paint a picture of despair -- I am only saying the trouble is very real. We are blessed people in a cursed world.

Those are her troubles. You must also be reminded of her value. There is, and will only ever be, precisely one of her. She was made to be exactly herself (and may fully become that, some day, as God is still working on her). Most importantly, she is worth no less than the death of God, because that is the current bid for her soul. I could never have time enough or words enough to really describe the miracle that is a woman of God. She is intrinsically beautiful and you should honor her because she is a lady. There are no exceptions to this rule -- in difficult cases, you must simply be a better gentleman.

(In case your head is full of stuffing, I feel compelled to point out that honoring a lady does not mean indulging her. If she is being stupid, honor may very well require that you *not* humor her).

ORIENTATION -- LESSON 3. A TOUR OF YOUR DUTIES

"I do everything that I am not told not to do."
-- Pearson Threepieces

Here is a very broad description of the duties which you must learn to execute with deadly efficiency. (You will not find this list precisely enumerated in Scripture, but you will find a commandment to Love. From what I know of my sisters-in-Christ, I believe these are effective ways to love them). A lady needs brothers to do the following:

- Serve her

- Protect her

- Affirm her, and

- Lead her (should anyone think to accuse me of chauvinism, I will thank him to read less of the space between the lines, and more of the lines themselves).

Attention will be given to each of these areas as we progress.

Do not underestimate the positive effect that a man (or better, a number of men) can have on a woman by treating her as special on pure principle, almost absentmindedly, without intending to gain something in return, as if it were simply natural that she should be well-treated. Conversely, do not underestimate the damage that a man can do by not valuing her, or by treating her like a commodity.

As is so often the case, neutrality is elusive. When two people interact, the net effect is rarely zero. If the people involved are a young man and a young woman, a net zero effect is almost unheard of. We had better try pretty hard to be a blessing, or we will almost certainly be a curse.

Do you understand the situation? As a brother you are responsible for taking care of your sisters. It is dreadfully important. In a time when so many are shirking that responsibility and ignoring their sisters or taking advantage of them, you are needed even more. The world turns on individual people trying their level best to protect what they love.

ORIENTATION -- LESSON 4. THE BROTHERHOOD

"Weep not for the lone maiden because of her peril, but weep for the men who are missing. My heart does not break from fear, you can see -- it breaks from shame."
-- Little old quotable me (is that cheating?)

I have always felt that life comes to me like a story. That is why I sometimes talk in storybook language. Now some of my favorite stories really do involve maidens isolated by severe circumstance, whipped by freezing wind on a mountaintop, facing down inevitable challenges. It is courage and loneliness enough to shatter my heart or set it soaring.

To put it in everyday language -- to tell you what breaks my heart in the story we are living -- I see Christian men who have either forgotten, or never learned, or chosen to ignore what it means to be a brother-in-Christ. I see a brotherhood that is not even prepared to treat women like ladies, let alone sisters. I see Christian women who do not even know how much we have failed them, who at best hope to be treated "decently". I see princesses who have never even heard of champions (or who believe that only a man "in love" can or should fulfill the role).

This should not be! Any gathering of Christians is a family gathering. When one of our sisters is with us -- with all of us, with any of us -- she should get a certain impression. When she thinks about us, her brothers-in-Christ, she should be able to think and feel certain things. Things like,

"They really care about me."

"I'm important to them."

"They think I'm special."

"I can depend on them."

"I can trust them."

"I'm safe with them."

"I'm welcome with them."
"They remember me."

"They take me seriously."

"They're honestly interested in my well-being."

"They pay such attention to me -- they really notice me."

"When I have something to say, they listen."

"They're so helpful."

"I'm glad they're praying for me."

"I know they'll stand up for me, even if I'm not around."

"They keep me sharp."

"They're gentle with my feelings."

"I've learned so much from them."

"They're a godly influence."

"They see God's banner over me and help me see it too."

"They're out to give, not to take from me."

"I can be myself around them -- I don't have to pretend."

"I'm stronger because of them."

"If I fall, they'll catch me."

"If I'm in danger, they'll protect me."

"If I'm lost, they'll find me."

"I'm glad to be around them."

"They put my needs and comfort ahead of their own."

"They believe in me."

"They're my friends."

"They love me."

"They're good guys."

"They're family."

Our sisters need us. If they can't say these kinds of things (and more) about us then we aren't fulfilling our responsibility towards them. But if we accept the responsibility, if we become brothers for our Christian sisters, we will bless their hearts and change their lives. The body of Christ will be strengthened, fellowship in the family of God will be deepened, righteousness will flourish, and the Lord will be glorified.

That's the moral of the story and the whole reason I'm writing, and I hope it sounds as magnificent to you as it does to me. The sad part is that the relationship between brothers-and-sisters-in-Christ has been pretty well neglected and underdeveloped. It ought to be something that transcends chivalry...but even chivalry is presumed to be dead (though it is not dead), and anything beyond it is barely imagined. Many girls do not believe in brotherly love. They are likely to regard any real display of it as nothing but the ghost of some long-dead honor -- or worse, a ghost-story.

And don't you know that in a world where the real things are all dismissed as ghosts, a thing must become ghostlike if it is ever to be accepted as reality? Hence all this sneaking, see...

ORIENTATION -- LESSON 5. FINISHING LAST

"Take a look at them. They're all nice guys, but they'll finish last. Nice guys. Finish last."
-- Leo Durocher

I happen to own a copy of a valuable letter, written by a man of no consequence to one of his sisters. I doubt it is worth any money, but it is worth a lot more than money to me because it is so true. Whatever imperfections the letter has, it is the best explanation I know for why a Shadow Gentleman must be Shadowy (which is not to say Shady), so with the lady's permission, I had better just reproduce the letter here instead of telling you all about it!

I haven't changed anything from the original except to conceal the name of the author and recipient, and to omit the more personal sections out of good manners.

My Dear Miss,

Consider yourself privileged, for you have the rare opportunity to read something that few, if any, female eyes have ever read. It is an ancient manuscript from the archives of the League of Mostly Ordinary Gentlemen. It contains trade secrets and arcane teachings, so of course I am trusting in your discretion. The ancient manuscript is attached as the next page in the letter. I am showing it to you because it explains some of the difficulties in attempting to be nice directly. The preferred method is to be sneaky and be nice without getting caught. The manuscript gives two reasons why sneakiness is recommended.

Pay special attention to the section on "Reflection". This is when a gift reflects well on the giver but is never truly accepted by the recipient. It is when the emphasis is placed on the "From Who" instead of the "To Who".

(He continues on a more personal note, but the part we are concerned with is the ancient manuscript! It is attached at the end of the message, written in a careful and scientific hand. I reproduce it for you here...)

```
                  Two Reasons Why Mr. Nice Guy
                    Must Learn To Be Subtle
         (or, Why It's Hard To Make Encouragement "Stick")
    --------------------------------------------------------
```

Reason #1: Basic Mistrust (often very valid)

1."Nice guys finish last."

   -- Common "knowledge". Often quoted, if not
      officially widely believed.

2.Selflessness of nice guys is recognized.

   -- "Wow, he's so nice and doesn't even mind
      finishing last!"

3."Nice guys finish NOT last."

   -- Willingness to finish last is rewarded by
      finishing not last (possibly due to feelings
      of obligation on the judges' part).

4.Selflessness of nice guys called into question.

   -- "If nice guys don't finish last, maybe he's being
      nice for his own sake after all."

5.Nice guys deemed not so nice after all, so finish
last (see step 1). Niceness rejected on suspicion of
ulterior motives.

Reason #2: Reflection (this is the tricky one)

1.Niceness is offered by a Nice Guy.

2.Niceness is recognized as such, & admired by
recipient

   -- "Why, how nice of him to do/say/think that!"

3. Point of gesture missed completely...

   -- "It couldn't be that *I* am deserving or worthwhile,
      etc..."

4. Encouragement reflected back at the Nice Guy.

   -- "...so it must be that *he* is very thoughtful and
      nice, to have done something like that!"

5. Niceness fails to have desired effect of giving the
intended target a sense of acceptance, assurance, worth.
Intended target may possibly just feel more unworthy.
Abort mission!

For these reasons, Mr. Nice Guy, you must be subtle. You
must smuggle in your niceties undetected. Your target
must realize that she is appreciated, but she must
realize it gradually! Be nonchalant, matter-of-fact, even
a little absent-minded. Draw no attention to yourself. If
at all possible, encourage her towards her own
conclusions instead of just giving her your conclusions.
She must believe, after all. Above all, do not act like
you know you are being nice. Then she may very well
suspect you have ulterior motives, or that you are nice
because you are great, not because she is.

But we know better than that, gentlemen.

                                        Best regards,
                                        N.G.

Hmm. I don't agree with *everything* in that letter -- for instance, the part about nonchalance. I am a big fan of plain old chalance, but we will talk more about that later. And I don't agree with his use of the word "selflessness" -- I much prefer "loving sacrifice". Anyway I agree with the man on all the points that I find agreeable, and that is enough. People might complain about finishing last, but it is blasted hard to actually do it! It is easy to get disqualified from the race altogether if a girl thinks you are faking brotherly love for any of many wrong reasons. Or you might accidentally end up in first place, which is almost as bad! It means that you have somehow gotten ahead of her.

No, what we want is that coveted position: Last Place. I prefer to call it the rearguard, a place that a humble man might be proud of, if he can only avoid being exalted for it.

ORIENTATION -- CONCLUSION

I hope that the last lesson confused you. That means you are starting to see the complications. Christian Love is usually pretty simple, though very difficult. Most of the time when we fail to love somebody, it's not because we are confused about how to do it. Like James says, we know the right thing to do, and we do not do it.

Loving our sisters is a little different. It's like trying to live out simple Christian Love while being tackled by a pack of monkeys, and all the monkeys are carrying those metal ring puzzles that you have to try to pull apart (you know, those puzzles wrought of pure frustration, that cruel relatives bring to holiday parties to make children cry; and when the children grow up they are never able to look at those puzzles again without feeling a kind of vague shame and casting about for a hacksaw; and even key-rings will never seem totally innocent again...) and you have to solve all the ring puzzles and wrestle all the monkeys to the ground before you can even get close enough to your sister to take a shot at Christian Love.

This is a hard saying; who can understand it?

Well I will tell you that it is a very profound metaphor for life, and since I just made it up, I will also make up a meaning. The monkeys represent the temptations and wicked tendencies in your own heart, which you must defeat before you can even see your sisters clearly. So things like disrespect towards women, or like thinking of girls as nothing except potential girlfriends, fall into this category. I do not trust monkeys.

The metal ring puzzles of doom represent the misunderstandings, lost memories and deep-seated fears that prevent healthy brother-sister relationships from happening in this strange world. The problems mentioned in the last section (suspicion and "reflection") are just a few of the puzzles we have to handle. A few others come to mind:

- sisters who in their "independence", resent our efforts to be brotherly

- the gossip that flutters and flies and gives our gentlemanliness a romantic connotation

- the tendency to interpret "guard your heart" as meaning "treat members of the opposite sex like potential assassins"

- the tendency to interpret "treat the younger women as your sisters, with all purity" as meaning "invest your emotions however you like, just don't touch her!"

With all these obstructive monkeys and impossible puzzles (I promise to not perpetuate this metaphor further), it would be nice to have some sound philosophy and some practical suggestions for finishing last. I can just hear you now, wishing for those things. By a sort of funny coincidence, that is exactly what you will get in the sections to follow.

You will continue to hone your skills as a gentleman ninja. You will continue to contemplate the nature of truth, humanity, and brotherly love. You will also learn highly efficient techniques for being nice to girls, and you will use those techniques to complete death-defyingly dangerous missions (did you think this book was all theory?).

Now you are ready to begin in earnest. Congratulate yourself, but don't overdo it. You have completed: Orientation! (And that's cool, right? Because ninja are like, from the Orient).

"Somebody must be terribly good, to balance what was so bad.

Somebody must be **needlessly** good, to weight down the scales of that judgment.

He was cruel and got credit for it. Somebody else must be kind and get no credit for it.

Don't you understand?"

-- Alan Nadoway --

(Four Faultless Felons, by G.K. Chesterton)

SERVE -- LESSON 1. THE FIRST STEP

"Do not hide from relatives who need your help."
-- Isaiah 58:7

We all know him, and many of us are him -- the guy who is quick to sympathize and slow to serve. The guy who will listen sadly to a sad story, who is interested in all of your problems...as long as he isn't part of the solution.

Don't be that guy.

On the other hand, don't be the guy who already knows all about your problems before you tell him, and knows exactly how to fix them in five seconds. Girls hate it when you do that (so does everyone else), and you will probably be wrong anyway.

Much better to be a good servant than to be either of these. A good servant will listen attentively and keep a sharp eye out for his master's needs. He will do all that is expected of him and quite a lot more, he will honor his master's wishes, and he will respectfully offer insight if he has it. "Good servant" might mean a thousand things, but always including this description -- he is USEFUL. He is occupied in meeting the needs of others.

There is so much to be said about serving. I could remind you that Christ set an example, showing us that Humility is inseparable from Service, and that Service is inseparable from Love. I could tell you how serving each other turns one person's problem into two people's joy. I could say a great many things and they would be worth saying, but I will be very strict and limit myself because I know that you can hear those kinds of things elsewhere, and stated very nicely. Wherever you hear such words, please pay close attention! Loving people is the second greatest thing you will ever do.

As for me, I am trying to say the things you might not hear anywhere else. And right now I want to stress this dusty, foreboding secret -- that sometimes, girls need help and you should help them. That sometimes, being a good brother does not require a hypersensitive heart or brilliant Bible knowledge, but just requires doing mundane tasks. I think you could be good at that.

See, service is integral to any kind of actual love, and usually we know that. But when it comes to girls we get distracted by all kinds of other things (like protecting, affirming, and leading them), and we forget that you can speak truth into your sister's life until your lungs collapse but it doesn't mean a shred of anything if you are going disappear at the first hint of being asked to babysit her sick cat! That kind of disappearing is using your ninja powers for evil. Shame on you. (And I have never actually babysat a sick cat...but after

23

writing this, you know it's gonna come back to me).

I am not talking about huge, crushing needs here. Those are actually not as much of a problem -- I think most of us are pretty decent in a disaster. "Your house evaporated? Well hey, if there's anything I can do..."

I am talking about being decent in the daily things. Sure, you can rise to meet a need. Can you sink to meet a need? If a girl broke her leg, you would carry her over a mountain. But if a girl sprained her ankle, would you weed her garden? If she was perfectly well, would you still look for ways to save her time or anxiety?

Service comes first in this book because it is different from the other sections. It does not sound Manly or Sensitive or Spiritual like the other duties we will discuss. It is not specifically a thing for brothers and sisters. The other duties might be new ideas, but service is so familiar that we are likely to forget all about it. We are forbidden to forget! Everything is important -- you know well enough yourself how all the little stresses of life can add up, and how wonderful it is when you can ask somebody for help.

But service also comes first because it is the necessary first step. You MUST be sincerely loving your sisters if you want to do any good at all. This can't be a hobby for you, or an act. Sincere love demands service, and service demands sacrifice -- so it makes a good test. Please don't try to lead your sisters or affirm them or protect them if you are not willing to serve them. Please ignore them altogether if you refuse to love them; you haven't earned them, and they deserve better than you.

In addition to being the foundational application of God's love, service is the foundation for all of your activity as a Shadow Gentleman. If you will permit me to use the word, service is your alibi. It is your perfect cover story, a kind of honest disguise. Yes, it is drudgery and dirty work -- but don't you know the ninja often went about dressed as peasants? And anyway, it is love. It will gain a girl's trust and free you from suspicion as you work towards further blessings.

A girl is obviously wise to be cautious when the world is so full of bad men. She is wise to watch everyone, even her brothers. That is why a trustworthy brother is such a precious gift, because he gives her a rest from all the watching.

A leader who is not a servant will just seem to be gathering followers for his own glory. Affirmation will sound like hollow flattery unless a servant speaks it. Even protection might seem like a kind of possession, as if you defended your sister in order to own her. But if she sees that your actions are really and consistently calculated to meet her needs instead of your own, you will have gained some credibility.

Your Lord was a servant -- so too must you be. But this book has a narrow scope, and a whole servant's heart will not fit inside. There are other books that will do you very well for service in general (like "Improving Your Serve" by Chuck Swindoll), and I hope that you read them...but I know you are not here for that. You are here to learn the ways of a Shadow Gentleman.

Now service (especially to sisters) does really benefit from our peculiar brand of sneaky chivalry, and that is what I will discuss in this part of the book. Like Jesus says, if you want to do it right, you have got to be a service ninja.

(For reals! Keep reading).

SERVE -- LESSON 2. SNEAKY SERVICE

"The funny thing is that most of us don't mind doing little or big things for others. We don't get hung up on doing it, we get hung up on being recognized for it."
-- Ordo Sanctus Chiros (sanctuschiros.org)

"Watch out! Don't do your good deeds publicly, to be admired by others, for you will lose the reward from your Father in heaven. When you give to someone in need, don't do as the hypocrites do -- blowing trumpets in the synagogues and streets to call attention to their acts of charity! I tell you the truth, they have received all the reward they will ever get. But when you give to someone in need, don't let your left hand know what your right hand is doing. Give your gifts in private, and your Father, who sees everything, will reward you."
-- Jesus Christ (Matthew 6:1-4)

Don't let your left hand know what your right hand is doing.

That's how Jesus says we should meet needs. Take a second to think about it. Imagine the greatest ninja you can possibly imagine -- whoa. That's a good ninja. BUT, I ask you this: can he hide from HIMSELF?

Because you see, Jesus says your hands should serve so quickly and inconspicuously that they never even meet -- they shouldn't even know what each other is doing. It's like...it's not good enough to just be one whole ninja. Your HANDS should be like little ninja on the ends of your arms; your right hand is off painting houses, your left hand is building dirt bikes for orphans and widows, and you're just sitting there like "What what? Am I serving? You don't even know!"

I am serious, in my own way. Forgetting yourself is a beautiful thing. I can almost never do it, and never without help. But that is the way we are supposed to serve. When someone asks you to pass the salt, do you do it with a flourish of helpfulness, or is it an unadorned, almost reflexive action? It ought to be reflexive even for greater things than passing the salt. If someone needs help, we should be moving before we think about it.

Please notice what Jesus does NOT say. He does NOT say that you should act like it's no big deal. We should never pretend like a good deed is not that great. Love is beautiful. It is not arrogance to do something loving and call it good. (Nehemiah is a good example of finding satisfaction in your obedience and not being afraid to admit it -- he who was humble and yet said, "Remember me with favor, O my God, for all I have done for these people"). What Jesus does say is that you should not walk around with a flashing neon halo and a sandwich-board sign that says "Servant, y'all". Jesus says that if you ask for admiration from people, you might get it...but that's all you'll get.

Be careful what you wish for, yeah?

So service needs to be sneaky -- actually sneaky, not the fake sneaky that is meant to make people look at you and say, "He's sneaking around, he must be doing something awesome." Just be cool. Remember that your reason for doing all of this is to live out God's love for your sister in powerful, practical ways. You want to fade into the background of the picture. You want your actions to say, "This isn't about me being nice! This is because God adores you and loves taking care of you -- and I agree with Him of course, but it's His Love. I just work here!"

(Incidentally, this section is supporting evidence for my theory that Jesus is the Best. Ninja. Ever. In addition to the whole service ninja hands thing, look at the entering locked rooms, the vanishing into thin air...not to mention defeating Death and all that...yep).

SERVE -- LESSON 3. SNEAK GOOD

This is not just about service, but I will mention it here. When I recommend sneaking, I do not mean it creepy-like. If your sister ends up thinking, "I don't know who this invisible helper is, but it's freaking me out!" then you have missed a few steps along the way, and probably caused a lot more anxiety than you have relieved. The easiest thing to do is think about what would happen if she caught you. If she would probably say "Aww, thank you!" then you are okay. If she would probably say "Err...what do you...think you are doing?" then you are being creepy. You should be honest, upright, and encouraging in your sneakiness, and not trespass against her property or privacy or personality (I did not choose those words for alliteration, but you will never believe that).

So these would be bad:

Showing up at a girl's dorm/apartment/abode while she is away, and asking her roommate to let you clean. Attempting to wash or fold her laundry in secret is also a bad idea. This is not respecting her privacy.

Also, moving heavy, valuable breakable things -- or doing any sort of tricky, fiddly operation without asking her permission. Even installing anti-virus software on the sly. This is not respecting her property.

Finally, you do not want to do things that disrespect her personality. Don't secretly help her in ways that just make her uncomfortable or upset. I say don't *secretly* do it. Sometimes you will have to oppose a girl's personality -- but you need to do that kind of thing *openly*. It is respectful to encourage a shy girl to speak up; it is possibly wrong to pull strings so she's unexpectedly in the spotlight. It is respectful to encourage a headstrong girl to let people help her; it is possibly wrong to go behind her back and "help her anyway" if she insists on working alone. Basically, sneaky things should be "I know she'll appreciate it" things. "I know you hate it but it's for your own good" things should be done (or suggested) out in the open.

And this would be good:

Your friend invites everyone over for pizza and games at her house. When dinner is over, you all go into the living room to play games. Passing through the kitchen on the way to the bathroom, you notice pizza boxes, paper plates, napkins and cups scattered everywhere. You are familiar with the house so you take a few minutes to toss the disposables, rinse out the cups and put them in the dishwasher. You also straighten up the chairs and wipe off the table, so everything is back in its proper order. Then you go back to playing games, and everyone thinks you just took a long time in the bathroom. They might not even realize there was a mess in the first place. Brilliant!

(But...some girls are really concerned about being a good hostess, and they would feel awful knowing that they "made someone else clean up", even if you are happy to do it. Service should not make a person feel awful, so respect her personality! If you want to clean, tell her that it would make you blissfully happy to do so, and ask if it is alright).

Now, a word about failure:

If you ever get caught while trying to care for your sisters, it is entirely okay. Sometimes it is unavoidable, and you can respond (either during the act or after the fact) with a straightforward "Happy to help! Thanks for letting me." I will admit that sneaking is an overcompensation, a shield against the suspicion that you are trying to make yourself look good. It does not really matter if you go noticed or unnoticed. You sneak to show that you *prefer* to go unnoticed. And this is your preference because it emphasizes your sister's welfare over your own glory.

And word about when to sneak:

NOT ALWAYS. In lots of cases you will need to let your sister know that you are available to help -- either because you need her permission in order to help, or because she is worried about something and needs to know that it is being taken care of. But even in these cases, let your work be characterized by humility. Complete the task without drawing unnecessary attention to yourself, and report your success joyfully but not smugly.

Remember that in all things, your aim is to meet your sister's practical needs in a way that helps her trust in and experience God's love for her.

Tips For Furtivity

These are excerpts from the short story "Becoming Invisible" by Jeffrey Clyde Sears. I read "Becoming Invisible" years ago and it changed my life (a little bit). Both men in the story have different motivations for becoming invisible -- one desires self-preservation, one desires entertainment. Our motivation is unique, of course, but that does not diminish the bizarre excellence of the story.

- Although seen by thousands of eyes, he prided himself in the well-timed misdirection, an effective bag of props, unadorned but pleasant apparel and an appreciation of the environment. It allowed him to stand safely within a crowd while everyone else was trying to stand out.

- "Compliment but don't clutter, you can still keep your identity, but do it quietly and smoothly." He let the last word "smoothly" drag out and added the universal downward-sloping palm-down hand signal for smoothly.

- "My realization began with the discovery that it really didn't matter what people thought about you or what other passive observation people made. Because being center stage rarely got me anywhere. Either I would grow exhausted by remaining on stage too long and disappointing the audience or I would grow resentful of the crowd."

- "My invisibility," I said, pausing for a dramatic effect, "must allow me to attend a grating social function or endure a claustrophobic shopping experience and come out unscathed. It also must allow me to wander through masses of humanity without disturbing traffic flows or the laws of physics."

  "And when asked about my involvement or participation in these social adventures," I continued, "people confirm my presence but they can't remember what I wore, said or did but they are almost positive that a good time did occur."

- "Quiet but pleasant looking shoes," he said while taking a final sip of coffee. "Squeaking shoes and the unfortunately memorable footwear available today will not help you at all. So purchase your footwear at the same place assassins purchase theirs."

- "Being invisible can be a state of mind but it is a moderately lame one if you still can be seen."

SERVE -- LESSON 4. PRAYER SERVICE

"The earnest prayer of a righteous person has great power and wonderful results. Elijah was as human as we are, and yet when he prayed earnestly that no rain would fall, none fell for the next three and a half years! Then he prayed for rain, and down it poured. The grass turned green, and the crops began to grow again."
-- James 5:16-18

About twelve minutes ago, I discovered that the Talmud (a Jewish religious text second only to the Hebrew Bible in importance in Judaism) calls prayer "the service of the heart". I adore this definition, and I would like to use it for our purposes. Shadow Gentlemen should always be wholehearted; what better than putting our hearts to work serving?

Intercessory prayer (or whatever the kids are calling it these days) is the easiest thing you will ever do. You are basically asking God to love His daughters (which He loves doing anyway), and you are asking Him to do all the work. And it is totally invisible! Nobody will know that you are praying for them unless you decide to tell them.

Intercessory prayer may also be the hardest thing you will ever do. It takes faith to believe you are making an impact. And it is totally invisible! That means no pretty smiles for your work, which will test your dedication to this shadowy career.

Please look at the opening verses to this chapter again. Please notice some important things about prayer. Prayer works...sometimes scarily. James is telling us the simple and very freaky truth that God responds when you pray. Have you ever seen a prayer fulfilled in front of your startled eyes? I have seen it. It feels like stomping the ground and hearing Earth say "Owch!"

Prayer has great power and wonderful results. This is because the power of prayer is the power of God. Do not worry that your prayer might have bad results! God knows best. Remember that you are praying to a loving Father, and that if you are silly enough to ask for rocks to eat, He will do you one better and give you bread!

Prayer should be earnest. That means, pray honestly and with all your heart. If you have not paid attention to your sister and do not know what she needs, tell God about that. If you are not sure your request is the best idea, tell God about that. But always make sure the prayer is centered on your sister and her needs. There is a time to pray about yourself, but not now (just like there is a time to read books for yourself, but not now! This is for them).

What about the necessity of being righteous? James is talking about the prayers of a righteous person after all. How should we understand it? If we have put our trust in Jesus, then we know He has made us clean. Are our prayers answered because of Christ's righteousness? Or is a life of obedience also required? I incline towards the former...but I really do not know. That is a book unto itself. All I will say here is that it does not change our direction either way. We know we must pray. We know we must obey. We know that we must pray even in order to obey. So we will do both, and trust God, and never be afraid.

Finally, notice that Elijah's prayer is very specific. Try to pray as specifically as your faith allows. It is good to pray for your sister in every way you can -- but the more specifically you pray, the more specifically you can praise God for His faithful response.

Above everything else, remember that the most important thing about your prayers is to pray them. Do not give up. God will use your honest offering -- but it must be offered!

I want to give you more than knowledge, though. More than pointers and instructions, I want to give you hope. If you are anything like me, you need an inspiration. So let me assure you that praying for your sisters is absolutely the most critical way to love them. Let me assure you -- it matters. It makes God happy and is a wonderful way to care for people.

It is so easy to say "I am praying for you" but it is so hard to stick to it. Let's be reliable for our sisters. I think that girls can sense a true man of prayer, because he has a kind of confidence in difficult times. "Let me talk to Him...this will all turn out right, see?" He is not afraid to pray for concrete things -- for little, daily things. (Riddle me this, is it scarier to pray for world peace or to pray for an extra fifty bucks?). Let's be the kind of brothers that serve our sisters in the most invisible ways, with our hearts as well as our hands.

In fact let's do it on the next page.

Sir,

There are times when it is appropriate to tell someone that you are praying for her -- in order to give her peace of mind and peace of heart, or in order to let her know that she is welcome to share her needs and joys with you. Sometimes, knowing that you are in another person's daily prayers is an absolutely tremendous blessing. But this is not one of those times. This is a stealth mission. You will bypass your sister entirely and go straight to the Higher Power on her behalf.

This is your first assignment because it is (and will remain) your most important. But also because it is almost impossible to mess it up. Talk to God about your sister and don't tell her about it -- can you handle that? I have supreme confidence that you can.

Eventually you will want to do this for all your close sisters, but for now choose just one. Do you have a crush on her? (I see your mind!) Choose another one. Disentangling brotherly love from romantic love is..."advanced". We'll talk about it in due time, be sure of that.

Have you chosen? Marvelous! Now this is a service project. That means you are aiming to be useful! Here we go...

Ask God to give you a thoughtful, Christ-centered view of your sister.

Reflect on what you know about her life and her self. Ask God to give you a true picture of her needs. Think about her needs for five minutes, and write them down as you think. (Time yourself! It is a good way to commit and to keep your thoughts from wandering. It helps you to say "I am doing this one thing, and this one thing only -- not eating, not answering the phone -- for this block of time." Five minutes is longer than it sounds).

Now this is very simple: spend five more minutes asking God to care for these needs. Pray specifically for each one, knowing that God is delighted to take care of His daughter, and delighted to answer the kindhearted requests of you, His son.

Do you know what you have done? You have quite silently and invisibly pleaded your sister's case before a Loving Power greater than the stars. Your prayers are useful, and God will use them. Who can say why the All-Knowing allows Himself to be moved by our ignorant cries? Because He loves us, I should think. Your prayers for her are an opportunity for God to love you both.

Commit to doing this every day. Five minutes for your sister in prayer -- and an extra five minutes at the beginning of the week to think if her needs have changed.

Thank you, sir! That's right gentlemanly of you!

Sincerely,
　　　　⟨there is no signature
　　　　...or else the author has an *invisible name*⟩

SERVE -- LESSON 5. FREE TIME

"Forget it. I don't want friends who won't be around tomorrow."
-- Squall Leonhart (Final Fantasy VIII)

"Therefore be careful how you walk, not as unwise men but as wise, making the most of your time, because the days are evil."
-- Ephesians 5:15-16

Before you proceed to seeing and serving your sister's needs, I want to make a very quick and important observation.

You will have noticed that praying for your sister takes some time. More sisters, more time taken, and that's just for prayer! When you start serving physically, you might get very busy. So think about this...

All of our time is borrowed, do you know? It belongs to the Lord! Be careful that you allow nobody else to own it -- not so that you can hoard it for yourself, but so you can give it away as a gift in His name.

It is difficult to be available for other people if your own life is spinning out of control. There are times when this is unavoidable, and that's fine -- that's when you need to fall back on the rest of the family.

But a lot of times, we are just overwhelmed by our own foolishness. Procrastination, poor planning, overreaching our capabilities. If you are involved in so many activities -- even so many "ministries" -- that you are brushing off people who need you, it is good to scale back. If you are a slave to last-minute projects, try to meet your responsibilities sooner. Be a servant of the Lord, not of laziness or self-entertainment or workaholism.

Do not always spring recklessly into action, but be *able* to spring. Time is one of the most precious gifts you can give your sister. Keep some handy in case she needs it.

SERVE -- LESSON 6. GATHERING INTELLIGENCE

"Enthusiasm without knowledge is no good. Haste makes mistakes."
-- Proverbs 19:2

If a real ninja is hasty and uninformed, he probably ends up getting eviscerated. The stakes are different for you, but still high enough. You run the risk of causing stress instead of relieving it, harming instead of helping, misleading instead of leading.

I cannot emphasize this enough -- you must be USEFUL, not just "polite". It is possible to be very polite and also be a complete nuisance. So you must know your sister's true needs, instead of what you imagine her needs to be. There are more than enough well-meaning idiots in the world already; you should try not to be one. If you want to serve, you must know what really needs doing and how to do it.

There are three ways to learn what she needs:

- Figure it out yourself. The Golden Rule applies, as does common sense. This is often the most direct and effective method, but it requires that you are not self-centered and that you have learned to be sensitive. Insight into human nature helps as well. You can get this by living with your eyes open and by reading old, good books, beginning with Proverbs and Ecclesiastes (in the New Living Translation of the Bible, if you enjoy a modern style).

- Learn from other people. Common sense may fail you when dealing with women, because they are basically counterintuitive. You can find these snags yourself, or you can save time and trouble by learning from the adventures of others. However, this is a good place to be on the lookout for well-meaning idiots. Even this book itself should be read with an alert and critical mind. A good rule of thumb is to pay attention to older married people that you admire. If possible, you may also wish to compare notes with other Shadow Gentlemen (or even workaday, ordinary Gentlemen), particularly those of a sympathetic and insightful nature.

- Gather information directly from the ladies in question, either by observation or through conversation. You should be able to gather everything you need without tipping your hand. And since you are solidly grounded in prayer by now (Mission Zero, yes?) you should be able to start gathering presently.

THE SHADOW GENTLEMAN'S ROAD
MISSION One -- WALLFLOWER

PRIMARY SKILLS REQUIRED
      Being-A-Ninja Skills: Going Unnoticed, Sidling
      Being-Nice-To-Girls Skills: Paying Attention, Iron Memory

Sir,

      This is an easy task and not very dangerous. It is suitable for a bumbling beginner like yourself. You will not be required to take special action, but you will be gathering information for use in future tasks.

      To begin, go about your daily activities as normal. This is crucial -- no one must suspect that you are up to something. In order to succeed, you must GO UNNOTICED, or at least no more noticed than usual.

      Your targets are the sisters that you encounter on a regular basis -- those that you see at school, work, church, or any other place that you visit consistently. (If you do not interact with any of your sisters on a regular basis, then you can go out of your way to find some...but I would rather have you find an avenue where you can be a reliable support to some of your sisters, and establish yourself there. A large part of being a brother is being a friend, which requires time and some measure of permanency. Plus, you will find it easier to GO UNNOTICED once you are well established).

      It is not necessary that you interact with these girls, but you should not attempt to avoid them either. Be natural. Your goal is simply to PAY ATTENTION. You are looking for clues about your sisters' needs and state of being. You may wish to focus on just one sister at first, or just one at a time, so that you can make a thorough job of it. Please choose someone other than the girl for whom you currently have romantic designs, so as not to unduly complicate the assignment.

      Many students at this point discover that they are habitually self-absorbed and that it is almost impossible to focus on another human being for an appreciable amount of time. You will need to overcome this difficulty with prayer and disciplined practice in order to complete the task.

      Use your EYES. Notice if she seems tired, happy, subdued, distracted, peaceful, jittery, or anything else. (When you have made a long practice of paying attention, you will be able to tell when she is acting out of character. This can be a valuable sign, but on the other hand, do not ignore her "normal" behavior either). Notice how she acts around different people, or in different situations. You may also wish to take note of her clothing, since it can give insights into her preferences and personal sense of style (this may not seem important now, but details like this are useful when you intend to care for people on an individual basis).

Use your EARS. How she sounds is important, but the first trick is listening to what she actually says. Again, you might (but might not) find that you have a difficult time tearing your attention away from your fascinating self to focus on what other people are saying. But it is absolutely critical that you hear what she says and REMEMBER it. Even light banter and aimless conversation will reveal what is on her mind and in her heart (or at the very least, tell you more about her current state of being and her distinct self). If she talks about what is actually happening in her life, be extra sure to PAY ATTENTION. You must take an interest in the people you are going to care for. This means that what is important to them becomes important to you (not that you have to agree with their priorities or desires, but you must be aware of them). Listen for anything that might be good to know in order to serve, protect, affirm, or lead her.

After collecting this information, commit it to MEMORY and slip away quietly. Excellent.

Sincerely,
⟨there is no signature, but you feel a slight breeze brushing by⟩

Tips For Furtivity

The trick to this task is that you must GO UNNOTICED, because your special interest in the girl would almost certainly be misinterpreted. You can not seem to be spying or eavesdropping. Indeed, because you are a Gentleman as well as a Shadow, you can not *in fact* spy or eavesdrop. You must be subtle, but not deceitful. Heed the following, and for crying out loud don't try to *look* furtive.

For watching:

- Glances from a distance are acceptable, but only if your target is in a public place and generally aware of your presence (though not aware of your attention). You do not want to intrude on her privacy. The downside is that you will not have long to observe, because a glance is naturally rather quick. Do not attempt more than a couple of glances unless you are more subtle than you think (doubtful). The idea here is that you appear to be watching nothing, but are secretly watching something.

- A potentially better option is to find a good vantage point and watch the *entire* scene. Watch every person in the room for a few seconds at a time, instead of just your target. Repeat as many times as necessary. Depending on your personality, try to look equally disinterested in everything (like a bored and imperious cat) or equally interested in everything (like a little yippy dog who is distracted by every noise and motion)...often the best way to look interested in everything is to in fact *be* interested in everything. But do not forget to focus on your target. The idea here is that you appear to be watching *everything*, but are secretly watching one thing.

- If she is talking to people, you may be able to join the conversation. Do this by making a passing comment (preferably relevant) and then sticking around, or by simply SIDLING up next to them and standing quietly until they believe you were there all along. Once you have joined the conversation you will be able to watch her whenever she is speaking (in fact it would hardly be polite not to). Of course you will have to watch the other speakers in their turn, as well. Do not try to infiltrate a conversation unless you are sure that it is public and that you will not be unwelcome.

For listening:

- It is recommended you SIDLE your way into a conversation (see above), or engage the lady in normal conversation yourself and PAY ATTENTION to what she says.

- Aside from participating in conversation yourself, take note of what she says to others when you happen to be nearby. If possible, happen to be nearby quite a lot, so as to catch more snippets. Just be discreet. Some people can sense a loiterer across a crowded room.

SERVE -- LESSON 7. PEOPLE ACTUALLY

"I don't deny the dry light may sometimes do good; though in one sense it's the very reverse of science. So far from being knowledge, it's actually suppression of what we know. It's treating a friend as a stranger, and pretending that something familiar is really remote and mysterious. It's like saying that a man has a proboscis between the eyes, or that he falls down in a fit of insensibility once every twenty-four hours."
-- Father Brown
  ("The Secret of Father Brown" by G.K. Chesterton)

By this point, if you are really following along and not just sitting like a literate lump, you have gotten a bit of experience in truly seeing and hearing these sisterly creatures for what they are. Even if you were caught and interrogated and grossly humiliated, take heart! All of your secrets are open secrets. You are not just honestly sneaking, but sneaking honestly, and sneaking for a lark (which is not to say a joke).

You should have noticed a curious thing: when considered as people, your sisters really do almost begin to resemble people. They might even start to look like persons -- individual, undeniable, living facts that are entirely outside of you but are still, somehow, faintly familiar. A good kind of strange...

Because of all that, this is a good time to remember what sort of needs a person might have, so you can do something about serving them. As you read, think about those glances and snatches of conversation you collected. Think about where those things fit into the whole picture of a person, and see if you can't surprise yourself.

A wiser man than me spent his life chasing after everything a person needs. He found out that none of it was enough by itself...but that doesn't mean the needs aren't real. He was wiser than you too, so it's probably best if we both listen. Reading his story (that's Ecclesiastes again), we see...

Wisdom is what your sister needs. Call it being in tune with reality. Call it reverence for God. Call it skill for living. Call it seeing what is hidden, or even more rarely, seeing what is plain to see. Call it all of those things -- your sister needs it because a foolish life is an awful life.

Happiness is what your sister needs. Fun is what she needs. Relishing life, appreciating all things good and beautiful. A kind of pleasant surprise at being alive. Wholesome, memorable moments and someone to call attention to them.

Purpose is what your sister needs. A direction to her actions, and knowing that her actions really matter. The opportunity to contribute to important, permanent things. Assurance that she is not just biding her time, that she really leaves footprints where she walks, and that her footprints will even become fossils.

Perspective is what your sister needs. Realizing her own role in the story of everything -- a small and critical role. Realizing that a whole month might revolve around a single minute...and that every minute will take its place in a whole month of minutes. Understanding that everything has its time, and experiencing the rude reminder that there's a world going on outside her own skull.

Rescue is what your sister needs. Oppression is a common thing. Cries for help are a common thing, and so is the silence of people who have given up even crying. But a man who will break the fangs of the wicked and snatch the victims from their teeth -- this is an uncommon thing, and all the more important for being uncommon.

Good company is what your sister needs. Traveling companions to make the hard road bearable, to help her succeed, to reach out when she falls down -- and to depend on her to do the same for them. Every person who ever lived had troubles they couldn't face alone, but two can stand back-to-back and conquer, and a cord of three strands can hold the weight of the world.

Provisions are what your sister needs. Don't dismiss food and clothing and shelter and medicine as mere material flotsam in a sea of high ideals. If these things are not high ideals in themselves, then being at peace about them certainly is. (As for the rest of the needs I have mentioned, they are as hard as hardtack...hardly an abstract sea).

Hope for life is what your sister needs. Hope that even hard times are sent to her with love. Hope that there is always a way for her to do the right thing, even when she is in trouble. Hope that there is always something new to learn, and that things are always moving forward -- not only in circles.

Hope beyond death is what your sister needs. Eternity has been planted in her heart, so she needs to know that death is not the end of meaning. She needs to know that she will never cease to be, and that there is love and real life beyond the veil. That for all the unpredictabilities of life, death is certain -- and that for God's children, the pains of death are labor pains.

Virtue is what your sister needs. God created people to do good and love what is right. Those who fear God will be better off, even when it seems like they suffer more than the wicked. There is always, again, a time and a way to do the right thing. A righteous life is a peaceful life, even when it is not easy.

Duty is what your sister needs. To keep her promises to God, to be entrusted with hard work, and to be measured against a high standard. Obedience to God, and to offices which have been granted authority by God. Obligation is something outside of herself. When she collapses, she can get back up for duty's sake. Duty destroys "I cannot" with "you must."

God is what your sister needs. The One who created her, planned her destiny and remembers her actions is also the one she must remember. Not next year or tomorrow. She must remember God today, before the silver cord snaps, before the water jar is smashed. The fullness of wisdom leads up to one thing: trusting this Person.

Ha ha, it is a lot, but you needn't be able to recite it. Don't be overwhelmed! Be just whelmed enough to understand that there are many ways, great and small, for you to help her.

That was the wide picture. Here is the narrow one -- we will start with her Practical Needs and postpone the rest.

What do I mean by Practical?

I wonder...

SERVE -- LESSON 8. TANGIBLE BENEFITS

"The highest does not stand without the lowest."
-- C.S. Lewis ("The Four Loves")

When the term "Practical Needs" is used in this book, it refers to those needs which can be met by offering physical provisions or a helping hand (and sometimes a helping mind). It usually means helping your sister get something done. Pages ago I said,

> *"Sometimes, being a good brother does not require a hypersensitive heart or brilliant Bible knowledge, but just requires doing mundane tasks. I think you could be good at that."*

That is what I mean by Practical Needs. I know our sisters have a lot of other needs, but we need to start with the "lowest". This is because the lowest are likely to be forgotten if they aren't put first -- and also because Practical Needs are not such a delicate operation, so they make a good starting point.

Mkay, side note aside! You will also need a good attitude while performing these secret deeds of service. Let's talk about chalance, because it makes me feel clever.

SERVE -- LESSON 9. CHALANCE

"For our boast is this....that we behaved in the world with simplicity and godly sincerity, not by earthly wisdom but by the grace of God, and supremely so toward you."
-- 2 Corinthians 2:12

Dictionary time! Merriam-Webster says that "nonchalant" means "having an air of easy unconcern or indifference." And maybe you think it is a good idea to behave that way. After all, we talked about not making our service into a big deal, right?

But no. Nonchalant and natural are different things. Very often they are contrary.

We want our sisters to know that it is only natural that we should serve them. It is Christ-natural -- in accordance with the nature of Christ. *In Christ and by His nature*, they are beautiful sisters who naturally deserve our brotherly love. Does this sound nonchalant to you? Or does it sound bright-eyed and boldly persuaded?

The good thing about nonchalance is that it's not heavy-handed. It doesn't jump forward and say "Look how I served you! I sure am doing my duty as a spiritual brother, yes? Yes." It just does a thing and moves on. Nonchalance is "easy unconcern"...and the "easy" part is really good.

The "unconcern" part is really bad because it is a lie. We most emphatically DO care about our sisters, and our actions should communicate this consideration, not mask it. Brotherly love can be subtle, but it must be honest. Love should be very sincere -- it "rejoices with the truth" (1 Corinthians 13:6).

(I know that ninja are renowned for the art of deception...but we are more than ninja. We are Shadow Gentlemen, and our art is more ancient and more powerful still. Our art is undeception, the opening of eyes).

This subtle, gentle sincerity is what I like to call "chalance" -- the inverse of nonchalance, obviously. Like nonchalance it is easy and breezy, but it is also decidedly interested, attentive and invested. I think we can say that if nonchalance is "having an air of easy unconcern or indifference", then chalance is "having an air of easy concern and real interest".

Nonchalance is like the silence between total strangers who don't want to talk to each other. Chalance is like the silence between old friends who both want to listen. It is natural and not self-conscious, but it is also intentional. It might be a sidelong glance, but it's a sidelong glance with a warm smile.

46

So when you serve your sister, don't act important -- but DO act like SHE is important. Don't fuss -- but don't trivialize. Be meek but not cold. Let your actions be expressions of truth.

And when she says thank you, don't say, "No problem." Say, "Any time," or "You're always welcome."

SKILLS REQUIRED
     Being-A-Ninja Skills: Prying
     Being-Nice-To-Girls Skills: Pleasantries, Chalance

Sir,

You have completed a general survey of your target. Hopefully you have spent some time in reflection, and you have a few ideas how to use these findings to her advantage. Nicely done. If you have an opportunity to put those ideas into action, pray and ask if you should take it. (You have my permission to act, but let's get that second opinion, yeah? Joshua 9 is left as an exercise for the reader).

The next step is to make yourself known. You don't want to reveal your secret superhero identity yet, but it is important to start interacting with her in a fraternal manner...for three reasons:

- If you have previously acted unworthily towards her, you have a lot of making up to do and had better start sooner than later.

- Part of her blessing in having brothers is *knowing* she has them -- so we have the unique challenge of being sneaky but also accessible, like a good butler. The similarities between butlers and Shadow Gentlemen are numerous, scary and wonderful.

- It is another excellent way to gather information about her needs and character.

So you must make small talk. This is easy for some of us and very difficult for others. My own mind is a leaky bucket when it comes to the daily details of my friends' lives. I can remember their virtues, vices, dreams and doctrine...but not their occupations, schedules, allergies and families. And it's hard to ask those questions, knowing the answers are going to be elusive.

But enough about me. If it's hard for you to keep track, keep a little book!

Make small talk, but do not make the mistake of thinking that small means trivial. Small talks are human love and fear in miniature, little snowglobe versions of everything we care about. Change something in the snowglobe and watch it shake the Earth. Archimedes said he would move the world if you gave him a place to stand and a lever long enough. Small talks are like a lever long enough...ish.

When you encounter your sister (either incidentally or by taking steps to do so), you should greet her and begin with PLEASANTRIES, which does not mean glossy smiles. It means talking a little bit about nothing. Why do we do it? To express our pleasure (hence "pleasantries") at meeting the person and speaking with her. We talk for a few moments about nothing -- a conversation with no content -- to show that we're enjoying the *person* herself and not just the *topic*.

Then it's on to the content, and with much CHALANCE (that's a light, easy attitude that still shows real affection and compassion), you will begin PRYING. Will you be my friend if I tell you a secret? This is the secret -- prying is mostly prying open your own head. Pry open your door and hang a "Welcome" sign out front, and most people will enter of their own accord. Loneliness or curiosity will compel them.

What I mean is, Be Inviting. Ask little, simple questions about things she cares about, and then she has the floor. If you don't know what she cares about, ask vague questions and let her fill in the blanks. My favorite one is, "What kind of exciting adventures have you been up to?" Ask a question and follow that line of discussion a while. Don't fire off questions or rapidly change topics. They're conversation starters, not bullet points.

You get to meet your sister! I hope you know what a great honor that is. You get to meet her on the common ground of the daily grind and learn how to help her, and that's a blessing to both of you, but especially to you.

Pry --

- yourself away from self-absorption.

- your ears open to hear her.

- your mind open to meet her.

- the doors and windows of your personality open, to greet her.

And when you have pried at yourself enough and you know how it feels, pry at her just a little bit. Mostly this means asking those simple questions and honestly caring about the answers. Normal people are pretty willing to talk about themselves, on some level, to an interested listener. There are a couple special cases that require special prying, but almost always, simple questions will do. "How is (life/school/work/your knee)?" Don't push for deeply personal right now. You are prying for practical needs! You are listening for ways to be helpful. Whatever interesting bits you hear, commit them to memory and write them down as soon as possible. When you have heard enough, wait until she glances away, then jump up and hide in the rafters.

Sincerely,
⟨the signature disappears in a blinding flash of cinnamon-scented smoke⟩

Special Cases for Special Prying

SPECIAL CASE #1: She is a talker. She'll have answers before you even ask questions. She'll tell you her past and her present and even her future without stopping for breath. If she talks that much, you might feel like you know a lot about her -- but sometimes (not always) people talk to cover things up. Pray and listen and sort through the chatter to find out what needs you can really meet. Listen for topics that come up multiple times, or topics that she is strangely silent about.

SPECIAL CASE #2: She is a closed book and you can't read her at all. Maybe she is too proud or too misguidedly selfless to let herself seem needy. For whatever reason, she is not willing to share her life. Consider using Sneaky Reverse Prying by sharing some of your own life. This is especially good when she sends the question back at you. "Oh I am having a fine day, fine, fine. How about you?" That is your cue to describe (shortly and sweetly) a few of your own joys and pains and thank her for listening. It gives her a chance to respond with a "me too!" story, or just to see that you trust her. And YOU get the bonus of having a sister listen to you and support you! Sneaky Reverse Prying indeed.

SERVE -- LESSON 10. SYNTHESIZE, PRIORITIZE

"Every act of will is an act of self-limitation. To desire action is to desire limitation. In that sense every act is an act of self-sacrifice. When you choose anything, you reject everything else."
-- G.K. Chesterton ("Orthodoxy")

You have returned, and with approximately the same number of appendages! I gather your encounter was successful.

Think about what you have seen and heard. Well, PRAY about it first -- MISSION ZERO NEVER ENDS, which is nice for us because we get to chat with God Almighty for ever. Can I say this too much? You are never alone. You are never acting all by yourself. You are working together with your Father to help your sister, and it is VITALLY important to talk with God continually about the girl you are trying to love. God's heart is for her very best, so keep listening to His heart.

Now you want to synthesize your information. First pray, "Please help me categorize her needs clearly and thoroughly." Then start figuring out what she needs, especially her practical needs, especiallier the needs you can meet, and especialliest the time-sensitive ones.

You already know what I mean by practical needs (from lesson 7).

But it's time to make choices between those needs. God has prepared many good works to be done...but not all of them to be done by you! Leave some for the rest of us. Embrace your finity and be -- emphatically be -- where you are.

Any particular need might be out of your reach, or out of your league, or out of God's will for you to meet. (If it is in God's will, league and reach will not matter). Do not assume that everything is your responsibility or even your privilege.

More probably though, you have the opposite difficulty. More probably, you want to shirk and slack. But you can't do that, oh no, no you can not! God has prepared some good works specifically for you to do. From what I can tell, a lot of them seem to fall into the following categories. You should definitely pay attention to:

- Needs that you are specifically *good at* meeting. For instance, I have a friend who is renowned for being able to fix anything, including but not limited to our sisters' high heels.

- Needs that you are in a perfect position to meet because of time and circumstance. Like when you sister needs a job and you are about to quit yours, you quitter, and can recommend her as a replacement.

- Needs that stick in your mind for God only knows what reason. These are the ones that punch you between the eyes despite your lack of good luck and expertise. Your only qualification is that you care very much. This certainly means you should pray hard, and might also mean that you should act.

Take note of the needs that stick out to you like this. But don't think you are above meeting her unremarkable needs either! There are a crowd of them, and they are all important.

But there is one more kind of Practical Need which I did not even list yet, because it deserves its own section. It is the most important of all.

SERVE -- LESSON 11. BEST AT A THING

"There are two ways to be Best at a Thing. The first way is to start by being a rare genius in your chosen field, and then to work very hard and practice every day and learn everything you can. If you are diligent and patient and lucky and smart (and nobody else is more of these things) then you might just become the Best.

The second way is to choose a Thing that nobody is doing."
-- Keys, of Par Posly

As you dwell on the ways that you can serve your sister, give special consideration to the things that NOBODY WANTS TO DO. The thankless jobs, or the ones for which "Thanks" is pretty paltry compensation.

These jobs are obviously necessary to do, because nobody is doing them. Do you want to be a useful brother? Do you want to bless her heart? Do you want to understand what it really means to be a Shadow Gentleman? Then do the difficult and necessary things without complaint, and without glancing around to see who notices.

(I laugh at myself for writing these words. My fingers are faster than my feet).

Our sisters have many very real and basic needs that are not being met because there is no glory in them for the servants...which says a lot about the foolishness of the servants. Lord willing, and He is, we will learn to be wise.

Look out for this kind of need, and do not hesitate when you think that you are not good enough, skilled enough or bright enough to meet it. Obviously you are not "too" good or skilled or bright to meet it. More than anything, you need to be *available*. Don't jump to conclusions (did you read Joshua 9?) but always be ready to pounce.

Pounce...good word.

Oh, I've made a sheet to help you sort out your thoughts, if you like that sort of thing. It is printed on the very next page for your convenience, along with an example sheet to spark your creative genius. (Write down everything that you know, and pray about which missions you should attempt to meet personally).

EXAMPLE -- Practical Things I Know My Sister Needs	Do it?
These are time-sensitive...	
Needs help calling a jillion people to invite them to a surprise party.	
Stranded on highway with flat tire (why am I sitting here writing?).	YES
Lost a dog. Find it.	YES
These are thankless and/or awful...	
Put away folding chairs after the meeting.	
Backyard is full of dog poop.	
I am great at these...	
Letter needs proofreading.	YES
Necklace need untangling (I am a grandmaster untangler).	YES
Needs someone to listen to stories of her stressful day.	
Making the most of ideal situations...	
Car is going in shop for a week. Needs a lift to her job, which I drive past every day.	
Wants to read "Hind's Feet On High Places". I own three copies. Give her one!	YES
Miscellaneous things I really care about...	
Is looking for good verses on Courage for a Sunday School lesson.	
Everything else...	
Cough syrup.	
Needs help choosing a good cheap laptop.	

Practical Things I Know My Sister Needs	Do it?
These are time-sensitive...	
These are thankless...	
I am great at these...	
Making the most of ideal situations...	
Miscellaneous things I really care about...	
Everything else...	

Tips For Furtivity

Sometimes your service will be impeded by fools and oafs and villains. One of their favorite traps is the bland, bleating phrase, "Oy! You ain't supposed to be here." What they mean is that they did not *suppose* you to be here...which obviously indicates a faulty supposition on their part. But most of them will not appreciate this line of reasoning. Better to avoid it.

You have heard of "hiding in plain sight"? It sounds like rubbish, but it can work. People often accept what they see, without question -- so do not give them a reason to question you. Make yourself at home. Act like you belong and most people will *suppose* that you do. This will not get you past people whose job it is to ask questions, but it might save you from people who ask questions as a hobby.

Think of how you act in a place where everyone knows that you do belong. Behave as such. For example, you don't burst boldly into your home like you have something to prove -- and you don't sneak in like a burglar either. Usually you enter purposefully or else absently, and treat most of your surroundings as a backdrop.

Not everyone is gifted with this talent. I am not very good myself. That is alright, because there are other strategies too. But this one is useful, satisfying, and worth practicing (someplace unimportant!). Just remember not to be selfish. You should care about the fools and oafs -- they are not your enemies. Do not distress them for pleasure or spite (indeed, never be spiteful). If you get caught, remember that you should not lie, but also that you are rarely obligated to explain yourself to people. Fail gracefully, recede peacefully, and retain your shroud of mystery.

THE SHADOW GENTLEMAN'S ROAD
MISSION Three -- BENEFACTOR

SKILLS REQUIRED
    Being-A-Ninja Skills:
        Puma Speed, No Survivors
    Being-Nice-To-Girls Skills:
        Respect for Her Privacy, Property, and Personality; Identity Theft

Sir,

    I am genuinely excited -- I have anticipated this moment, when a new brother (that's you) moves to ease our sister's burdens. She will benefit. If all goes well, you will be largely forgotten, except by God who sees all ninja and their deeds.

    At this point you should have a sister in mind to serve. You should have a list of her needs, and an idea of which need you will choose for this mission. For now, choose only one -- focus your strength. Act on a small scale so that you will not be detected. Act on a small scale, remembering Aristotle's lever.

    Wrap yourself in prayer, love, and silence, and set to work! Without knowing what need you chose, it is hard to advise you specifically -- but I trust you. More than that, I trust God who appointed you.

    Draw no attention to yourself. If you do attract attention, accept it with chalance.

    RESPECT your sister's privacy, property and personality in the way you serve her. Aim to make her strong and joyous. Aim to make God famous.

    Serve wholeheartedly and do your VERY best. Work as hard and as carefully for her as you would for yourself. Better yet, act like you are serving Jesus -- because you are! "And the King will say, 'I tell you the truth, when you [fed, clothed, welcomed, remembered] one of the least of these my brothers and sisters, you were doing it to me!'" (Matthew 25:40)

    Work with SPEED and PRECISION, carefully but quickly. Do not rush, but recognize that time is a gift from God. Save it so you can savor it. Work efficiently because your sister will be blessed when you are finished. Also to redeem your time, start as soon as you should. Don't procrastinate. She needs you.

BONUS CHALLENGE: can you do it without leaving any surviving witnesses? I don't mean you should kill people. That's messy and amateurish. Just complete the service and slip away without ever getting credit...if you think you're up to it. (I understand that some needs are difficult to meet in anonymity without being creepy. Use your best judgment, but remember those bonus points!)

Meet back here at 4:00 for juice and pretzels.

Sincerely,
   ‹a shadowy foot sails into your peripheral vision
   ...when you regain consciousness, the signature is gone›

SERVE -- LESSON 12. JUST ASKING

"Call this Shunammite....Say now to her, 'Behold, you have been careful for us with all this care; what can I do for you?'"
-- Elisha (2 Kings 4:12,13)

This is where we stop talking about service, but it is not where you stop learning. Continue to cultivate an unselfish servant's heart. Take a final lesson with you...

Part of being invisible is knowing when to jump out and say BOO! Or HYAAAGH! or your exclamation of choice.

Of course the invisibility needs to happen first. How are you going to leap from the shadows with much theatricality, unless you have first blended into them? So there are several invisible ways to find out how to serve your sister. Prayer, observation, careful listening, intuition, common sense.

But then there is Just Asking -- direct, visible, brilliant in its simplicity.

"I wondered, can I help you in any which way?"

Good question, that one. Better than "Do you need help?" (which may imply she just can't handle things on her own) and better than "Do you want help?" (which is less like offering assistance, and more like prompting her to ask).

"Can I help you?", asked in a hopeful tone, lets her know you will actually be pleased if you can help, which makes the offer easier to accept. It communicates an availability and eagerness to serve, which will be appreciated even if she has nothing for you to do (at least she will know she is not alone, and has someone to count on).

It is hard for a girl to ask for help if she feels like a burden. "What do you need?" puts the spotlight on her neediness. "What can I do?" makes her needs seem like gifts to you, assignments that you desire. (Which is indeed a miracle of the servant's heart -- troubles when shared become mutual blessings).

I do not say that Just Asking should replace other ways of knowing how to serve. A good servant is always observant (servant, *ob*servant, it almost sounds like I did that on purpose). And I do not say you should ask the direct question all the time, or any old time. We are not ninja for nothing!

You will have to discern when to Just Ask. When you have good reason for believing she could use the help (perhaps she makes a general comment about things going to pieces) but have no idea where to step in, then make the inquiry -- "Is there any way I can help you?"

60

SERVE -- CONCLUSION.

Hello sir. I am glad you are still here (I mean that). We brothers are always outnumbered -- every man counts! So you are a servant now, and you have learned these beginning lessons.

I will not give you another service project, because we need to move on to protection and beyond. I will not give you a project, but I will give you a charge: Serve always. Be vigilant. Finish strong.

Your sisters will always need things. There are always opportunities for the Praying Man to pray and the Working Man to work...which is good; else we would get bored! So please understand that serving is your permanent privilege.

Walking the Shadow Gentleman's road this far, you have quietly consulted with the Lord about one of your sisters. You have prayed for all of her needs and worked to meet one. Maybe you have even found some healing for the schism in your soul, that gaping breach between the Great Desires.

You have walked this stretch of road a single time. Now patrol it faithfully, for every sister, for all her needs, for the rest of your life. (I said that Mission Zero never ends...I forgot to mention that none of them end).

Again, you are not infinite, and not all good works in the world will be done by you. But what I want you to realize is that servants and brothers are not contractors. You cannot work a job and take your pay and skedaddle. Are you a (wannabe) ninja or merely a (wannabe) mercenary? Be loyal to your Family and to your Master, wherever He sends you.

Now we turn toward the more obviously brotherly duties of protection and affirmation. These will be difficult and dangerous and tricky and epic, which I am sure is exactly how you like it.

Ponder this graceful segue, and prepare yourself...

GRACEFUL SEGUE. SILVER AND CEDAR

In the Song of Solomon 8:9, the brothers of the bride-to-be are talking about their sister and they say, "If she is a wall, we will build on her a tower of silver. But if she is a door, we will barricade her with planks of cedar."

Up rises the wall, formidable, graceful -- all beauty, ready for battle. This Kingdom city will not fall, will not fail, though assailed by every evil. And above, towers of silver shining, flying the brotherhood flag. The worthy wall is honored, its loveliness accented, its strength bolstered. A tower of silver is a crown and a shield, a defense and a decoration. How do you build towers of silver? By nurturing godliness, praising true beauty, protecting innocence, defending goodness. The wall is strong already -- else it would not warrant towers, could not even support towers. The tower is the final touch of radiance and resolve, adding brightness to brightness in a grand celebration. And anyone looking at that mighty militant cheerfulness may be sure that the wall is not unmanned. So to speak.

What of a weak wall, a crumbling wall, in fact an open door? Towers cannot be built without a base...we must take a different approach with our stumbling sisters (and what sister is not stumbling, sometimes?). Planks of cedar -- to be strong for her when she is not strong. To brace the door against aggressors and keep her safe in the firelight of restoration. The daylight and triumph and trumpets will come later with the raising of the wall. For now, there is the battering of the door, the creaking (but not cracking) of the cedar beams, and the long siege.

Notice that cedar and silver both are rare and precious. We give our best resources no matter what. Bracing doors might seem hopeless...raising towers might seem needless. These seemings are just seemings. We have a little sister and she ought not to stand alone; we are her brothers with cedar and silver. There is building to be done.

"She has brought truth and you condemn it. The arrogance!

You will not harm her, you will not harm her ever again."

-- Kreia --

(Star Wars, Knights of the Old Republic II:

The Sith Lords)

PROTECT -- LESSON 1. CHAMPIONS

"Out of the mouth of the Mother of God
Like a little word come I;
For I go gathering Christian men
From sunken paving and ford and fen,
To die in a battle, God knows when,
By God, but I know why.

"And this is the word of Mary,
The word of the world's desire,
'No more of comfort shall ye get,
Save that the sky grows darker yet
And the sea rises higher.' "
-- King Alfred
   ("The Ballad of the White Horse" by G.K. Chesterton)

Wherever there is a lady, a princess, a sister of ours -- nearby there might be a mighty man, shining in his armor. By strength of arms and strength of voice does he throw back the darkness in folds. A paragon of valor, a ward against all fear, a bulwark never failing to impress.

Yeah, that's not us. But we probably do not need to hurt him, so long as he keeps a respectable distance from our sister. There are greater dangers under this dark sky than Prince Charming. I do not know if the sky is growing darker...it is enough to say that it is dark. The sea is high, whether or not it is rising. I cannot say if our sisters are harder pressed in this age than in any other -- but they are embattled for certain. Foolish people, wicked men and evil spirits are oppressing our sisters, using them and hurting them. Not cool, man, not cool.

Now listen to me. God is her shield and shelter. I will not paint a picture without that Light. It is not our job to save her, for she is ultimately safe. Nor is it always our job to keep her from sorrow and suffering...such troubles often bring growth (please, please read "Hind's Feet on High Places" by Hannah Hurnard for a sweet story about this).

No, when I say that brothers ought to protect their sister, I mean that we should fight to keep her *free* and *strong*. Exactly what is meant by freedom and strength will be discussed in later chapters, as will the exact threats to be faced and fought.

This is the immediately important point -- to keep a sister free and strong we must be willing to do the quiet, careful work of war. There will undoubtedly be loud battles and ugly skirmishes along the way, but sometimes the most ferocious fighting is done in silence. Being Shadow Gentlemen and all, we are mostly invisible allies and we do not step into the limelight for nothing. The element of surprise is precious to us! Sometimes your sister will not even know how much you fight for her, but at the right time she will know how much you love her.

Let us be realistic. Our sister has already been touched by the violence of sin, and we are therefore not fighting to protect perfect peace and innocence. We are fighting to *reclaim* it, and to protect what has been reclaimed. Now if we are fighting for peace, it behooves us to fight as peaceably as possible (that's another subtle skill for us to discuss).

There is the real difference, yes? Fight for peace and God's glory, and you will either become legendary or all but forgotten. Fight for the glory of battle and you will only become a celebrity...which is not as good as being legendary, and is even worse than being forgotten.

PROTECT -- LESSON 2. PEACEMAKERS

"Blessed are the peacemakers, for they will be called sons of God."
-- Jesus Christ (Matthew 5:9)

"'Blessed are the peacemakers,' not merely the peace lovers; for action is what makes thought operative and valuable. Above all, the peace prattlers are in no way blessed. On the contrary, only mischief has sprung from the activities of the professional peace prattlers, the ultrapacificists, who, with the shrill clamor of eunuchs, preach the gospel of the milk and water of virtue and scream that belief in the efficacy of diluted moral mush is essential to salvation...in actual practice they advocate the peace of unrighteousness just as fervently as they advocate the peace of righteousness."
-- Theodore Roosevelt (America and the World War)

In order to fight for peace, we must understand this blessed occupation of peacemaking which characterizes the sons of God. As Mr. Roosevelt points out, the blessing is for those who MAKE peace. It is not enough to like peace, to approve of it and say that it is generally a good idea and oh, someday, I hope to see it fill the land! No. Peace is made through actions of lovingkindness, not through sunny thoughts.

But we know that our own souls are a battlefield! How can people like us become peacemakers? The answer is in Jesus Christ...

> *"[Jesus] was delivered over to death for our sins and was raised to life for our justification. Therefore, since we have been justified through faith, we have **peace with God** through our Lord Jesus Christ."*
> *-- Romans 4:25-5:1*

There are no seeds of peace in our heart unless they are planted by faith in Christ. There is no way we can produce our own peace -- but it is one of the fruits that grows out of a close relationship with God. You must depend on the Prince of Peace for everything.

The peace that He gives is not a mere cease-fire (where violence ends for a while, but hatred remains). Nor is it simply turning a blind eye to festering wounds. It is true reconciliation of the kind which enables old enemies to embrace and honestly call each other "friend".

We usually think of peace as the absence of hostilities and other bad things...but the Bible uses a much richer word, full of positive meaning. It is the Hebrew word "shalom", and according to the Brethren Revival Fellowship:

Not only does shalom convey the negative -- the absence of strife and evil -- but also the positive, the presence of all good things. To wish shalom on another was in essence to say, "I wish for you not only the absence of all that may harm, but also the presence of everything that makes for a person's good."
-- brfwitness.org

This is the peace with God that we have experienced! The presence of everything best for us. Now that we have received so much, it is our place to become givers. Peacemakers.

Think about your role as a defender and protector. Are you fighting towards a true and lasting peace? Too often, victories only pave the way for more trouble.

- Seeds of resentment still linger from the American Civil War.

- The Treaty of Versailles, signed at the end of the First World War, exacted harsh vengeance upon Germany, which contributed to German poverty and discontent and to the rise of the Nazi party.

- Absalom's "protection" of his sister (by murdering the man who had raped her) led to bitter estrangement from his father, a pointless revolution, and his bloody death. (2 Samuel 13)

How can we avoid this?

Firstly, by praying. Thank God for the peace that He gives and ask Him to make you a peacemaker. If you are headed for chaos, He will correct you.

Secondly, by being sure to love your enemies and your sister's enemies, even while fighting against them.

Thirdly, by being committed to the truth in all things, because truth (even hard truth) brings peace to those who accept it.

Fourthly, by honestly desiring peace. I know that it is nice to feel needed -- but the dream of every true protector is unemployment. Fervently pray that perennial flowers will bloom wherever your blood is shed.

And finally, you can be a peacemaking protector by recognizing that your sister still needs to fight her own battles -- as we will discuss, curiously enough, on the following page.

PROTECT -- LESSON 3. SUPPORTING CHARACTERS

"Bear one another's burdens, and so fulfill the law of Christ....But let each one examine his own work....For each one shall bear his own load."
-- Galatians 6:2,4,5

"And what is it you think you have accomplished? If you seek to aid everyone that suffers in the galaxy, you will only weaken yourself...and weaken them. It is the internal struggles, when fought and won on their own, that yield the strongest rewards. You stole that struggle from them, cheapened it. If you care for others, then dispense with pity and sacrifice and recognize the value in letting them fight their own battles. And when they triumph, they will be even stronger for the victory."
-- Kreia (Star Wars, Knights of the Old Republic II: The Sith Lords)

There is such a thing as a crippling defender, who weakens a thing by guarding it. The classic case is an overprotective mother sheltering her children, but a brother-in-Christ can be just as guilty. I have been just as guilty.

When I was young and foolish I struggled from a need to be needed. I was afraid to protect my sisters too well, lest they become free and not need me anymore. I liked having lots of disasters to deal with, because it made me feel useful and valuable. I forgot that it was not about me, and I forgot that brothers and sisters can enjoy each other just as much in sunny weather as in a storm.

So I tried to handle *everything*. I should have been saying, "God willing, I will be strong enough to help you regain your strength and freedom." But I lost sight of the goal and said, "I will be strong so you never need to be." I took "bear one another's burdens" in an unhealthy direction, which gave my strong sisters a reason to stop confiding in me at all, and gave my weak sisters a chance to become hyperdependent. And at the end of the day, I protected nobody very well.

Insecurity, then, is one way to become a crippling defender. Pride is another way -- forgetting that you yourself are blessed by the opportunity to protect her. Misplaced kindness is another way -- thinking that your goal is to keep her in a sublime, rosy bubble, safe from every kind of sorrow and suffering.

Instead of these, be a nurturing defender. Guard her in order to help her grow! It's not a difficult concept, but it's difficult to know where to draw the line. How do you stand up for her without stealing her thunder? It helps to remember that you are a secondary character in her story. She is the protagonist, Christ is the hero, and you are buried somewhere deep within the credits between "Second Bus Driver" and "Groggy Talk Show Host". So what will you do with your few seconds of screen time?

73

Yes, you must protect her physically. But in doing so, have you made her more timid? You should have encouraged her to stand up for herself in the future!

Yes, you must protect her mentally. But in doing so, have you only insisted she agree with you? You should have helped her to learn to think clearly and love the truth!

Yes, you must protect her spiritually. But in doing so, have you increased her fear of (or fascination with, or skepticism towards) demons? You should have called her back to God's perfect protection, and helped her to see that she is weak in herself but invincible in Christ!

We do not want the fragile victories of brute force, but the robust victories of true wisdom, transformation and reconciliation. Just like us, she must have difficult experiences and see the truth in God's eyes.

Still...to be always saying, "You'll have to do this on your own -- it's the only way you'll learn!"...that's just obnoxious. Should we really dispense with pity and sacrifice? No! But save your pity for what is really pitiable. Do not pity her because she must fight battles (that is noble!). But if she is forced to fight those battles bound and blindfolded, then by all means pity (and therefore protect) her!

Hmm. All these words about overprotection, but so many of us struggle from the opposite impulse. Many of us are likely to underprotect, to say "it's not my business, don't get involved" -- because getting involved might make you seem overprotective!

That is part of the reason I have made a big deal out of it. I want you to understand that there is a difference between "protect" and "dominate". You can humbly protect your sister -- you can serve her with the strength God provides, and you can do it in a way that makes her stronger. Now, I do not currently have the time or wisdom to write a detailed guide to avoiding overprotection. You'll have to do this on your own -- it's the only way you'll learn!

But I can leave you with this observation: that I am sometimes called to protect my sister *from* a struggle, but far more often called to protect her *through* it.

I quoted Kreia at the beginning of this chapter. She is always worthy of close attention, but should be taken with a pound of salt. All these thoughts on overprotection were inspired by her warning:

> *"Be careful of charity and kindness, lest you do more harm with open hands than with a clenched fist."*

PROTECT -- LESSON 4. WHAT IT MEANS TO BE FREE

"Freedom's not found in the things that we own,
it's the power to do what is right."
-- Michael Card
  (lyrics from "The Things We Leave Behind")

This song by the inestimable Michael Card contains my favorite definition of the word freedom -- the power to do what is right. The power to *choose* what is right and by the same token, the power to choose something else.

This is no place for a full treatise on free will, but I will briefly mention that one of the distinguishing features of humanity -- one of the ways we are made in God's image -- is our willpower and our ability to work our will on the world. Our free will (a gift from God) also makes possible many of the most important and beautiful things. For example, love and obedience depend on free will, because love and obedience are choices.

When you hear about freedom, you are probably inclined to ask "freedom from what?". This is good as far as it goes, but it does not go nearly far enough. You should be asking "freedom *for* what?". Nobody would care about escaping from a prison if the whole universe was just prisons inside of prisons inside of prisons. There is a world outside that is better than the cell -- a place to escape to, something to be free for.

Jesus talks about freedom, as in the following passage:

> *Jesus said to the people who believed in Him, "You are truly my disciples if you remain faithful to my teachings. And you will know the truth, and the truth will set you free."*
>
> *"But we are descendants of Abraham," they said. "We have never been slaves to anyone. What do you mean, 'You will be set free'?"*
>
> *Jesus replied, "I tell you the truth, everyone who sins is a slave of sin. A slave is not a permanent member of the family, but a son is part of the family forever.*
>
> *So if the Son sets you free, you are truly free."*
> *-- John 8:31-36*

In this conversation, Jesus mentions a very peculiar and important thing about human beings: we are never really our own masters. Oh, we want to be, but we cannot be. We were not created for it -- we were created to serve and worship the Lord. Even when we choose not to serve Him, we can not get away from our role, so we end up serving and worshiping something else. "I am my own man" is a lie...anybody who is proud enough to try to rule himself ends up being ruled by pride. Everyone who sins is a slave of sin, "for a man is a slave to whatever has mastered him" (2 Peter 2:19). "Don't you know that when you offer yourselves to someone to obey him as slaves, you are slaves to the one whom you obey -- whether you are slaves to sin, which leads to death, or to obedience which leads to righteousness?" (Romans 5:16)

There is one way out of slavery to sin, and that is through allegiance to Christ. If (and only if) the Son sets you free, you are free indeed. Free for what? Well, to "become slaves of righteousness" (Romans 5:18) -- which is a wonderful thing to be! It means that you are right where you belong, and your heart can find rest.

Paul talks about the purpose of our freedom when he says, "You, my brothers, were called to be free. But do not use your freedom to indulge the sinful nature; rather, serve one another in love." (Galatians 5:13) We are set free to choose love!

This is the kind of freedom that you should desire for your sisters -- to see her wholly surrendered to a liberating Master as opposed to an oppressive one. Now that Jesus Christ owns her, she will never be separated from His love! (Romans 8:38-39) But she might be bullied or enticed into acting like a slave again -- forgetting her freedom and reverting to old fearful habits. Much of what we do as brothers and defenders, then, is to remind our sister of how free she really is and to sharply contradict anyone who says differently.

Please realize that being freely and fully surrendered to Christ means a lot more than just "not sinning anymore". It is a life-transforming choice that can only lead to ridiculous, exhilarating adventures, too much heartache to swallow, too much joy to stand. It is a Real Life, at long last. May our sisters fully realize this Life and claim it! It is the power to do what is right.

And while we're quoting song lyrics, here are some more I like, from the song "Free" by Ginny Owens:

> *Free from worry, free from envy and denial*
> *Free to live, free to give, free to smile*
>
> *You're free to dance --*
> *Forget about your two left feet*
> *And you're free to sing --*
> *Even joyful noise is music to Me*
> *And you're free to love*
> *'Cause I've given you My love*
> *And it's made you free*
> *I've given you My love*
> *And it's made you free*
> *I have set you free*

PROTECT -- LESSON 5. TAKE HEART AND BRACE YOURSELF

"I have told you all this so that you may have peace in me. Here on earth you will have many trials and sorrows. But take heart, because I have overcome the world."
-- Jesus Christ (John 16:33)

Jesus was right (fancy that). Here on Earth we do have many trials and sorrows, and so do our sisters. Christ talks about peace and victory. The question for us as brothers-in-Christ is this: how do we get involved?

I believe that brothers are created purposefully to be defenders. This duty takes many forms; there are many angles of attack and defense. But the goal is always the same -- to bear the brunt of the onslaught, form a protective hedge, break various chains and keep our sisters free (and to not get captured, ourselves!).

What onslaught am I talking about? What in this world could captivate, enslave or hurt our sisters? We will break it down, but please understand...we are fighting for peace. It is good to be innocent and ignorant of the darkness. Even though we walk through the valley of the shadow of death, even if we walk wrapped in darkness, we should not ingest it or take it into ourselves or make it a part of us.

"If you gaze long into an abyss, the abyss will also gaze into you," said Nietzsche (even a blind squirrel finds a nut once in a while). We will learn to recognize evil, but we will not meditate on evil or put it first in our thoughts. Christ's overcoming love and power is our theme song.

So this is our study pattern as we learn to become mighty men of valor:

- Meditate on the Good Thing :)

- Recognize the Bad Thing :(

- Fight the Bad Thing >:(

- In order to get back to the Good Thing. ^__^

If you will humor my thirst for very broad categorization, our sisters ought to be able to enjoy:

- Freedom and Strength of Body

- Freedom and Strength of Mind

- Freedom and Strength of Spirit

77

And they are in danger of being captured or crushed by:

- Violence

- Lies

- Temptation

We should also uphold justice, which does not fit prettily into any of these categories, but sort of spans all of them.

That's the sketchy overview. Lock and load, brothers.

PROTECT -- LESSON 6. FREEDOM OF THE BODY

"Murder, mountain-climbing, hugs, handshakes, kneeling, sneaking, or dancing -- actions mean more than just their physical facts. What you do affects you on a deeper level because it is the whole person, not just the body, who acts."
-- Jakeb Brasee's "Apoblepo"

A Shadow Gentleman should be very attuned to the connection between body and spirit. He of all people should realize that some things are felt before they are seen. It is a lie to say that physical things do not have spiritual value! "The blood of Christ" is not a metaphor, you know. You might find this lesson slightly mystical; your mind likely wants a bit of stretching, then.

God takes a very keen interest in human bodies. First He decided to make them, which is weird enough. In the Old Testament, He instructed His people in bodily purification to help them understand spiritual purification. In the New Testament, His Son brought things full circle and said that the inside of the cup is more important than the outside, that pure actions spring from a pure heart, not vice versa.

And then something astonishing happened: God decided to move in...

> *"Yet the body is not meant for sexual immorality, but for the Lord, and the Lord is for the body.*
>
> *Do you not know that your bodies are members of Christ?*
>
> *Or do you not know that your body is a temple of the Holy Spirit who is in you, whom you have from God, and that you are not your own?*
>
> *For you have been bought with a price: therefore glorify God in your body."*
> *-- 1 Corinthians 6:13, 15, 19, 20*

These verses are talking about our literal, physical bodies (as evidenced by the mention of sexual immorality). From a warning about sexual sin, Paul transitions into a deeper truth that touches all of life. That truth is that the Spirit of God dwells in our bodies, therefore every physical action -- not only sex, but eating, drinking, and whatever else you do -- should be dedicated to that Spirit and should please Him. (1 Corinthians 10:13)

A true house of praise and dedication should be filled with joyful, faithful worship. Truth should be spoken there, and righteousness should be lived out in honor of God. Sacrifices should be made willingly as required, and the doors and windows should be open so that the sound of singing can be heard even far away. This is what a temple ought to be -- not a place where the priests are at war with their own God (or just as badly, where they ignore Him).

And so the Bible says,

> "Therefore I urge you, brethren, by the mercies of God, to present your bodies a living and holy sacrifice, acceptable to God, which is your spiritual service of worship."
> -- Romans 12:1

Many translations of this verse end with something like "which is your reasonable service." The idea being that you don't give out gold stickers just because a person honors God with their body (just like you don't give out gold stickers when a barber trims your luscious locks -- because if he refused to fulfill that role, it would be *unreasonable*). This verse is saying that because God has been so merciful to us and because He is God, it is only right for us to respond with worship, obedience and willing surrender.

Is a temple really free if it is trying to remain independent of its deity? Hardly. Well, you might call it free in that case...but you could never call it a temple. The only way to be free AND to be a temple at the same time is to be utterly surrendered to a liberating Lord.

Remember what Jesus talked about? It is the inside of the cup that makes it dirty, not the outside. There is not much we can do as physical defenders to keep the temple clean -- that happens on the inside, and it depends on her willingness and the work of the Holy Spirit. Even in physical captivity or physical violation, when the temple of God is assaulted, she can stay free. In the words of Augustine of Hippo:

> "since no one, however magnanimous and pure, has always the disposal of his own body, but can control only the consent and refusal of his will, what sane man can suppose that, if his body be seized and forcibly made use of to satisfy the lust of another, he thereby loses his purity?" (The City of God, Book 1, Chapter 18)

Augustine goes on to say (and I agree) that if purity could be destroyed by another person's actions, then purity would not be a spiritual virtue at all. Instead, he says, it would fall in the same category as strength and beauty and health and "all such good things as may be diminished without at all diminishing the goodness and rectitude [righteousness] of our life."

In other words, purity is a choice, and can only be lost by a choice. A temple can only be defiled from the inside, though it be outwardly defaced and destroyed.

80

But still...but still. Our sister's master is God Himself. Nobody else. Yet many women are pressured to surrender the power to do what is right with their bodies. And if anybody does deface that beautiful temple whom we love, if anybody tries to set himself up as her false master, or tries to restrain her from touching the world with joy -- will we tolerate it? Oh I think you know the answer to *that*.

PROTECT -- LESSON 7. GO BIG OR GO HOME

"It is great being a guy because you get muscles just by going through puberty."
-- Mr. Jonathan Oesterman

A ninja is a finely tuned instrument of imminent doom. He is the first-chair violin in a symphony of destruction. Body, mind, and spirit -- unified and sharpened to a razor edge for one deadly destiny. Everybody knows that.

Shadow Gentlemen are by necessity a little more well-rounded (sometimes very literally). But the fact remains that most of us have the ability to be, if not Samson, at least not Delilah. If we are talking about protecting a sister from physical harm and oppression, then it is reasonable to say we ought to be physically strong.

Physical strength is of course the least among the strengths -- it is a virtue that we share with the beasts. But if eating and drinking can be done to God's glory, I believe it is true for exercise as well. If the lion's strength testifies to the glory of God, why not your strength? As King David sang in praise, "He trains my hands for battle; he strengthens my arm to draw a bronze bow" (Psalm 18) and "Praise be to the Lord my Rock, who trains my hands for war, my fingers for battle" (Psalm 144).

These days it is not very fashionable to mention any real differences between men and women, but I never had my fingers on the pulse of fashion except when I was strangling it, so I am willing to make this very radical statement: Men are physically stronger than women.

I will be the first person to admit that I know a few girls who could probably beat me up. So I acknowledge that my radical statement is not universally true, but it is true in the overwhelming majority of cases.

Most men have been entrusted with more physical power (or at least more potential for it) than have most women. I say that if we do not make good use of our potential by staying fit and strong, we waste what God has given us, and we fail to be very useful to our sisters in this way.

I do not here have time to recount the stories of Joshua, Gideon, Samson, David, Jashobeam, Eleazar, Shammah and all the other ridiculously beastly warriors in the Bible. I must settle for saying that God is not above using a bit of muscle to work His will, and I will point to one very good story from Exodus chapter 2, which goes like this:

After Moses had killed an Egyptian (bad use of strength!) and fled to Midian, he sat down beside a well to rest...

"Now the priest of Midian had seven daughters who came as usual to draw water and fill the water troughs for their father's flocks. But some other shepherds came and chased them away. So Moses jumped up and rescued the girls from the shepherds. Then he drew water for their flocks."

Granted, it does not say *how* he rescued them, but the 1956 Charlton Heston classic film "The Ten Commandments" has a very stirring battle scene at this point in the story. A starved and dehydrated Moses rises up from the bushes where he had collapsed, and beats down the shepherds with a big ol' staff. Good use of strength! And notice how he continues to *serve* them by drawing water after he has *protected* them. Incidentally, everyone should watch this movie at least once in their lifetime. So let it be written, so let it be done.

He stood up for seven sisters who could not stand up for themselves, and it was his physical prowess and bravery that enabled him to do it. There might come a day when you face a similar challenge, when you will need to match strength for strength with evil men for a sister's sake...or lift something heavy, or run a great distance. God knows, but who else knows?

(Moses got a meal and a house and a wife out of the deal, too, but I am not promising you anything).

I do not say that every one of us should devote ourselves to weightlifting and martial arts and firearms (although it gladdens my heart to know that there are some such people in the brotherhood). And I realize that for some of you, an unavoidable frailty holds you back -- in which case you are in good company! In 1 Timothy 4:8, Paul writes to the young pastor (who suffered from frequent physical infirmities) and says that "while bodily training is of some value, godliness is of value in every way, as it holds promise for the present life and also for the life to come."

And yet, bodily training is of some value -- if for nothing else, then for protecting our sisters, and that should be enough. And we cannot leave it up to the very strongest among us. Every man should take responsibility for his own body, and should try to be strong and fit for his sisters' sakes.

So I say to the great majority of you, to those who could stand to get off the internet and move around a bit, who have foolishly surrendered themselves either to shrimpiness or obesity or shapelessness, who have not gotten far past the default musculature that Mr. Oesterman speaks of...to you I say, go big or go home! (Whatever that means...) Work at least to be healthy and fit.

Consider also if you ought to learn techniques of defense (or as I do, flail a stick around in the back yard and pretend to be Faramir). If you are small or weak, do not be dissuaded. You can be quite as useful in a scrape as your more thuggish brothers, by focusing on quickness, subtlety, and shots that count. If you are timid, do not be discouraged. Pray *for* courage!

God is our ultimate source of strength, and I do not say that we fight by our own power. But out of thankfulness for our bodies and consideration for our sisters, let us be prepared to move in this world.

Now I sit hunched over my laptop in the basement, writing these words, reflecting on what has been a very sedentary life. This chapter is calling me to be better than I am. It would be ironic at best, hypocritical at worst, for me to wave a scrawny fist and send others off to the war.

So I am running around a lot, picking up heavy things, eating green things -- and I find that even in the absence of a crisis, the change is markedly pleasant.

Go and do likewise! If you fail in this matter, the sisterhood cannot compensate for the loss.

PROTECT -- LESSON 8. THE BUMBLING BODYGUARD

"Christianity is a fighting religion. It thinks God made the world -- that space and time, heat and cold, and all the colors and tastes, and all the animals and vegetables, are things that God 'made up out of His head' as a man makes up a story. But it also thinks that a great many things have gone wrong with the world that God made and that God insists, and insists very loudly, on our putting them right again."
-- *C.S. Lewis (Mere Christianity)*

"As a sex, women are physically weaker and less sexually and physically aggressive than men, and so they are far more physically and sexually vulnerable than men. This is not rocket science. But it's the reason that in our culture, as in all civilized cultures, honorable men historically have felt a moral obligation to use their advantage for a good purpose, to protect women from physical danger. Especially when that danger presented itself in the form of dishonorable men."
-- *Betsy Hart (Jewish World Review, August 1, 2000)*

This is the part of the book where I confess my ignorance and include long quotes at the top of the page as compensation. I know nothing about physically fighting to protect our sisters -- I have never (knowingly) been in a situation where it was necessary, and I would not know how to respond in such a situation.

On this subject, I can go no further than I have gone. I have attempted to describe the wonderful worth of physical freedom, and I have encouraged you to be peacemakers even while being warriors. I have urged you to be as prepared for the defense as possible -- but I cannot speak to the defense itself. I have given you no missions in this area because I am unqualified: a fledgling student.

Well, all of us have the Holy Spirit then, so let us pray that God will teach us. There are books and websites about the relation between Christianity and Martial Arts -- I plan to read them and see if they are talking wisdom. I can only beg you to do the same. Our sisters (and all women) need the protection of strong and honorable men, and I intend to become one. Though I feel shaky and hesitant and aimless, this glorious anthem is ringing in my ears: "I said I'd get my sister home in one piece, didn't I?"

Moving along then! If I have little to say about physical protection, I have much to say about the battlefield of the mind. We have spoken of Strength, and now we turn our thoughts toward Truth.

(Note: It is especially tricky to deal with the truth about your sister's own value and identity. I have called this Affirmation and given it a main section unto itself, following Protection).

PROTECT -- LESSON 9. FREEDOM OF THE MIND

"Not only do we know God by Jesus Christ alone, but we know ourselves only by Jesus Christ. We know life and death only through Jesus Christ. Apart from Jesus Christ, we do not know what is our life, nor our death, nor God, nor ourselves. Thus, without Scripture, which has Jesus alone for its object, we know nothing, and see only darkness and confusion in the nature of God, and in our own nature."
-- Blaise Pascal (Pensees)

"Like the sun at noonday, mysticism explains everything else by the blaze of its own victorious invisibility. Detached intellectualism is (in the exact sense of a popular phrase) all moonshine; for it is light without heat, and it is secondary light, reflected from a dead world."
-- G.K. Chesterton (Orthodoxy)

Life hangs on God like a coat hangs on shoulders -- everything falls into place. Life makes sense. The universe snaps together with a satisfying "click". I do not just mean the physical universe, but all of human experience, emotions, dreams, struggles.

We are made in the image of God, and our powers of thought are one way that we resemble Him. He gave us intelligence so that we could reason truthfully and appreciate the orderliness of His creation. But human intellect, removed from the Lordship of Jesus Christ, is used less for *reasoning*, and more for *rationalization* of our stubborn sinfulness.

On the other hand, human intellect submitted to the Lordship of Jesus Christ is a magnificent thing. King Solomon knew this. When the Lord appeared and said to him, "Ask what you wish me to give you," then Solomon replied, "I am but a little child; I do not know how to go out or come in....So give your servant an understanding heart to judge Your people to discern between good and evil." And the Lord was very pleased! (1 Kings 3)

Solomon did not know very much, but he knew enough to know he didn't know enough. So he did what any of us should do -- ask God to make us wise, and then do our best thinking for Him. And Solomon had pure motivations, wanting to judge his people fairly.

Doing our best thinking requires dependence on God, thankfulness for the gift of intelligence, and a willingness to glorify Him in our mental activity. (Just like freedom of the body, remember? The mind is not free unless it is joyfully surrendered to the Loving Master who alone is strong enough to protect it). And our motives need to be pure, or else our guilt will keep us from thinking honestly. But even though human intelligence is good and God-given, it is not good enough! We need something...divine.

"we speak wisdom among those who are mature, yet not the wisdom of this age, nor of the rulers of this age, who are coming to nothing. But we speak the wisdom of God in a mystery, the hidden wisdom which God ordained before the ages for our glory, which none of the rulers of this age knew; for had they known, they would not have crucified Lord of glory."
-- 1 Corinthians 2:6-8

For the Christian mind, wisdom is not simply something to satisfy curiosity or bring prosperity. It is a revelation of the Spirit, by which we understand "the deep things of God." God has prepared so much for those who love Him! How can we ever comprehend it? We can comprehend it because "we have received, not the spirit of the world, but the Spirit who is from God, that we might know the things that have been freely given to us by God" (1 Corinthians 2:12). Could we ever adequately describe God's love in terms of mere reason? Never! The angels, for all their intelligence, still long to look into the mystery of the Gospel -- but the stupidest human can come to understand it, by the Spirit, by living within the mystery. (1 Peter 1:12)

Fools perish for lack of wisdom...and for our world's lack of wisdom, God's Own Fool* perished, "for had they known, they would not have crucified the Lord of glory."

I suggest that the pinnacle of wisdom is to worship, revere and love the resurrected Lord of glory. This wisdom begins with the fear of God (Proverbs 1:7). It leads to fearing nothing else, and basking in His generosity.

Now, "the man without the Spirit does not accept the things that come from the Spirit of God, for they are foolishness to him, and he cannot understand them, because they are spiritually discerned" (1 Corinthians 2:14). But does this mean that God's wisdom only applies to our spiritual life? Does it transform our devotions and leave our daily business untouched? Hardly!

"The spiritual man makes judgments about all things, but he himself is not subject to any man's judgment:

> *'For who has known the mind of the Lord that he may instruct Him?'*

But we have the mind of Christ."
-- 1 Corinthians 2:15-16

The mind of Christ.

Spiritual discernment in all things.

Knowledge of God's great gifts to us.

You would not crucify the Lord of glory -- you would tremble in fear and adoration.

This is what happens to a mind once God has got His place in it, and above it, and has brought it into His kingdom, and renewed it by His Spirit. No longer plunged into darkness, such a mind will find new light flooding every corner and will discover wondrous truth in the most trivial or pitiful concepts and experiences. And does it make a difference? In a single Bible verse, Paul summarizes freedom of the mind very neatly and tells us the excellent results:

> "Don't copy the behavior and customs of this world, but let God transform you into a new person by changing the way you think. Then you will learn to know God's will for you, which is good and pleasing and perfect."
> -- Romans 12:2

We should earnestly hope for our sisters-in-Christ to enjoy this freedom, this power to do what is right with their minds! But the pattern of this world is deceptive and tempting, and if we are to be good brothers, we must encourage our sisters, protect them on the mental battlefield, and hold fast to the wisdom of a better kingdom.

---

* "God's Own Fool" being one of my favorite references to Jesus, learned from the song of the same name by (who else?) Michael Card.

SKILLS REQUIRED
> Being-A-Ninja Skills: Seeing The Unseen
> Being-Nice-To-Girls Skills: Receptivity

Sir,

Please enjoy this leisurely reconnaissance mission. Scope out the situation, to be sure, but also take time to see the sights in the landscape of lies. Please send me a postcard, but do not drink the water. (In all seriousness, yes -- I drink Pepsi).

As a first step in upholding your sister's strength and freedom, you must discover if the wisdom of this age has gained a foothold in her life. Maybe she is vulnerable to certain lies -- maybe she is still copying the pattern of this world. Or maybe she is standing strong but is exposed to lies every day and does not have a lot of shelter.

Pray for discernment, then begin a conversation with her. Talk about anything -- family, entertainment, money, politics, theology, food, favorite books, or whatever comes up. Keep it light-hearted, but search deep enough to find out these things about the topic:

- What she believes

- How she lives

- What motivates the way she lives

Be pleasantly RECEPTIVE, because you are just scouting. Keep a curious tone, asking questions simply for the sake of discovering what she thinks. Ask questions with enough chalance to keep her from feeling interrogated. If asked, freely share your own point of view (this encourages her to do the same) but remember that the goal is not to change her mind at this point.

I hope that the conversation is enjoyable and enlightening. Drift back into the shadows for a period of reflection. What circles of thought does she travel in? How does her mental landscape look? Lies will not always be lying on the surface. They may be buried, unseen assumptions, but ask God to make you able to see them. Ask yourself:

- Are there any areas of her life where she is obviously buying into the world's viewpoint?

- Are there any areas where she knows God's way, but faces a lot of pressure to go another way?

Commit these areas to memory (or cleverly, resourcefully write them down). You have gained a better understanding of what particularly threatens your sister, so that you can pray very specifically and take decisive action...soon, soon.

Sincerely,

‹AH-HA! you snatch at the signature -- but it is just a convincing straw dummy›

PROTECT -- LESSON 10. GET REAL

"Could you dish me up a little more pudding, there's a dear. And a spoon, then? I never eat pudding with my hands, or (for the same reason) win quarrels through cleverness, or earn love by any means."
-- Pearson Threepieces

Consider the issues.

What issues? The issues at hand!

You will need more hands to count all the issues.

We are often tricked into compartmentalizing our thoughts, sectioning off each area of life. So you will hear people saying, "It's not personal, it's just business" -- as if each shard of a man's life is governed by a different set of rules. This is a divide-and-conquer strategy. The enemy wants to convince us that our allegiance to Christ is irrelevant to "the issues".

This, of course, fragments us. And we can make the same mistake in trying to protect our sisters. If we only "consider the issues", we are treating the symptoms instead of trying to keep her healthy.

Please, don't get me wrong. There are times when somebody believes a very particular lie, and needs that lie to be destroyed by clear, strong reasoning. That is why I am very grateful that God has raised up defenders of the faith in specific fields. It is good to have people who can answer the false claims of secular psychologists, archaeologists, sociologists...dentists.

But we are not all experts, and in a lot of cases, our sisters are smarter than we are! They can grow in the Spirit's wisdom, just like us. If they want the facts, they can study for themselves.

Good news! You do not need to be intellectually superior to become a mental protector. You do not need to be an expert, or even very bright, though you should always do your best thinking for her sake.

No, a Shadow Gentleman works much closer to the source of thought, out of the limelight, far beyond the issues, beneath the waves. A Shadow Gentleman works to support his sisters' *worldview.*

What is a *worldview* and why is it *italicized*? According to FAQ for The Truth Project (from Focus on the Family), a personal worldview is defined as "the set of individual truth claims which I embrace so deeply that I believe they reflect what is really real -- and therefore they drive what I think, how I act, and what I feel."

A Biblical worldview, they say, is defined as "a formal worldview based ultimately upon that nature, character, and being of God as it is expressed in His infallible Word and His creation. It becomes the foundation for a life system that governs every area of existence."

If our overarching attitude or approach to life is solid, then all the little issues won't knock us around so much. We will be able to tell when some particular lie does not fit into the big picture.

Obviously, it is outside the scope of this book to discuss a comprehensive Biblical worldview. For that, I highly HIGHLY recommend The Truth Project (website: thetruthproject.org) if you can attend the seminar or somehow acquire the DVD's. Indeed I cannot recommend it strongly enough.

Here are some questions that should be answered by a Biblical worldview (these too are borrowed from The Truth Project):

- What is Truth?

- Who is Man?

- Who is God?

- What is Scientifically True?

- What is the Significance of History?

- What is the Proper Role of Family, Church, Community, State, and Labor?

- What is the Proper Relationship Between God and Man?

- Am I Alone?

- What Is My Purpose?

So maybe you can't change your sister's mind about an issue. Maybe you don't even know if her mind should change. But you can always repeat the fundamental truths of life (God's existence and power and character, Christ's love for us, our obligation to love and obey, et cetera) and help her think about what those Big Ideas mean in all the little parts of her life.

It's not about being the smartest person in the room. It's about recognizing that our minds are under attack, and being alert. Don't accept things without testing them! Set up a filter for incoming ideas. Actually think critically instead of swallowing cultural slogans.

While others are (praise God!) arguing brilliantly and directly for righteousness in the issues, we are working from the other side -- softly brushing the big picture, making ripples, gently suggesting the most foundational assumptions.

Keep up a continual hum of basic, life-changing truth. Any brother can do this, and all of us should. Why do we keep silent about truth when we talk to our sister? In a landscape of lies, sometimes all she needs is a little change of scenery.

THE SHADOW GENTLEMAN'S ROAD
MISSION Five -- A CHANGE OF SCENERY

SKILLS REQUIRED
> Being-A-Ninja Skills: Subliminal Message
> Being-Nice-To-Girls Skills: Giving Time

Sir,

TIME is a gift from our patient God. You should be patient too, and appreciate time. It is a necessary ingredient in the changing, growing, and healing of a human being -- and now you are going to learn to use it.

Did you talk to your sister as instructed in the previous mission? Hopefully you gained some insight into her mental landscape and discovered where she most dearly needs defenders. Now your first instinct might be to sit her down and tell her where she's misunderstanding the truth...but that's not how we do.

Remember that you are still trying to remain invisible. Remember also that you are working to nurture a deep peace in your sister's heart -- a peace that will not be shaken by the next lie (or hundred lies) that rise up. So instead of attacking the issue itself, start quietly introducing truth into her life. Do not call attention to it or to yourself! The truth will make itself known if you place it somewhere visible.

An example will help: Suppose your sister is deceived into thinking that abortion, in general, is not terrible. And suppose that modern dogmas of Tolerance and Choice and Convenience have blunted her discernment so that you cannot reason her back to rightness. How should you protect her mind?

Firstly by praying that she will grow in the Spiritual wisdom we discussed earlier. And secondly, by changing scenery! Be the person who speaks sincerely about the blessing of children. Openly admire those parents who raise kids in difficult circumstances. Praise God (out loud!) for the idea of family. Make quiet observations about how precious is this or that person, especially children. Abortion thrives in selfishness -- so you be the person who upholds sacrificial generosity.

These should be SUBLIMINAL MESSAGES. In the example above, don't be obviously referring back to abortion (actually, all of the blessings of children and family are plenty good enough to talk about *without* an ulterior motive). Exposing lies is a separate challenge, but your goal for now should be to bolster your sister's defenses -- her knowledge and love of truth -- so that lies once exposed cannot survive. Think of ways to improve her mental backdrop, and start immediately!

Changing the scenery is great because anyone can do it. It does not take a genius to talk about what is good and true. It just takes a brother who isn't embarrassed, and who is willing to be patient. That's the other thing. You cannot tell how long it will take for truth to bloom. Plant the seeds, and water them faithfully...but trust God to make them grow. Give it time.

Sincerely,

‹you stake out the empty space, thinking the signature cannot hide forever›

Common Lies Your Sister Might Believe -- and Subliminal Messages to Undermine Said Lies

- "If you accept people for who they are, you find out they are basically good."

  o Reflect on the man you used to be, and praise God for changing you.

- "Evolution is a proven fact, and Creationists are unscientific."

  o Learn to be awestruck by creation, and express your wonder at how it reveals God's glory.

- "My friends would not like me if they knew who I really was."

  o Be vocally glad that Christ loves us with all our problems, before we get cleaned up!

- "Christianity has a totally shameful, violent history."

  o Take time to discover the truth (pleasant and unpleasant), through books like "Christianity on Trial: Arguments Against Anti-Religious Bigotry", "How Christianity Changed the World", and "How The Catholic Church Built Western Civilization"...share interesting tidbits that you never knew.

- "It doesn't matter what kind of movies I watch, 'cuz they're not real!"

  o When invited to watch a movie that glorifies sin, refuse

with a cheerful, humble explanation that you would rather spend the time doing something that celebrates goodness...and then DO that something!

- "If I could go back to the Good Old Days of 30 or 100 years ago, everything would be fine."

  - Speak hopefully of Heaven and the loving reign of a truly perfect King.

- "I'm scared to look too closely at the Bible, 'cuz it's full of contradictions."

  - Tell her how Biblical wisdom has made a difference in your life and has never let you down.

- "Judging other people's actions is wrong (except for judging their judgmentality)."

  - Admire something good that a person has done. Remark how grateful you are that they chose to do that good thing instead of something bad!

This is not a list of lies and refutations. It is a list of lies and sneaky ways to slip the truth back in! I realize the list is very brief...I do not like to dwell too long on all the dangers of the world. I much prefer to worship the Lord who keeps us safe, but even He has told us to be wise and wary. For a more comprehensive look at the lies which threaten your sisters' freedom and strength, I heartily recommend the books "Lies Women Believe" and "Lies Young Women Believe", by Nancy Leigh DeMoss and Dannah Gresh.

PROTECT -- LESSON 11. THE BEST DEFENSE

"Fallacies do not cease to be fallacies because they become fashions."
-- G.K. Chesterton

"At any street corner we may meet a man who utters the frantic and blasphemous statement that he may be wrong. Every day one comes across somebody who says that of course his view may not be the right one. Of course his view must be the right one, or it is not his view."
-- G.K. Chesterton (Orthodoxy)

By changing the scenery and introducing truth as a backdrop, you create an environment where lies seem out of place and cannot grow easily. But there is also a time for direct assault and the snapping of chains. When lies have already gotten a grasp on your sister and are pulling her down, you should strike repeatedly and with force until she is free -- just be sure to strike the chains and not the girl wrapped up in them.

Your qualifications: you have the Spirit, you have God's Love, and you are an outside observer, which is important because the inside of a blindfold is almost invisible.

Your weapon of choice: the Sword of Truth, the Word of God, which is able to judge the thoughts and intentions of the heart. (Hebrews 4:12) Do not say you are too dumb to beat a tricky lie. The Word of God always makes a difference! (Isaiah 55:11) I have said it already about the physical realm -- protection is not just the province of the powerful! Quoting Scripture is something that every brother can and should do in the face of lies.

Lies are, ultimately, destructive because they are contrary to the nature of God. For example, God sees and values a person's heart. We contradict God when we make physical appearance the most important thing. That is why superficiality is a lie and a sin -- because it disagrees with Truth Himself.

So obviously, quoting Truth Himself is a pretty good way (and ultimately the only way, ha) to destroy lies. Have faith in God's abilities, not your own!

Since you are armed with such a mighty weapon, you should attack boldly! Learn and love the Bible. With it, you can show your sister that she does not need to be trapped and enslaved by any lie. You can show her that the lie does not match up with what God is really like.

Say what you know, not what you think. It is good to have Absolute Truth, because the last thing she needs when she is in danger is your opinion.

SKILLS REQUIRED
Being-A-Ninja Skills: Hiding Behind the Sword
Being-Nice-To-Girls Skills: Bible Knowledge

Sir,

It is easy to be passively invisible. Far, far more difficult to leap to your feet, slash through a web of lies, set the world on fire with Truth and still go unnoticed. But how if every eye were fixed on the Sword in your hand, so dazzled by the flame that they never remembered who held it? Today you will be hiding in plain sight, behind your Sword.

Ask God if there is a lie for you to slay. Maybe a lie that your sister has already bought, or maybe one that is just waiting for an entrance. God will protect her -- but quite possibly, through you.

If so, ask Him to teach you the Truth you will need. Prepare yourself by reading the Bible. How does God speak against this lie? Maybe you will only be able to think of broad, sweeping truths -- but such truths are mighty! Please resist the temptation to get fancy. The most powerful words might be, "God Loves You", "God is Everywhere", "God Can Do Anything", or "Jesus Has Saved You From Sin".

You have already been cautioned to strike the chains without hurting the girl, if at all possible. This means you attack the FALSE IDEA, but you do not attack her for being deceived. Remember that she is a prisoner of the lie. Pity her -- she is your sister, not your enemy. (Later you will learn to lead her further into Truth, but for now you will simply focus on setting her free).

So wait for the topic to arise, or chalantly stir it up yourself. Say you have been thinking, especially thinking about what God says. Humbly share what God has said, and give Him credit! Emphasize those parts that are clearly in opposition to the lie she believes. (Be ready to show her in the Bible, just in case she asks). This is not a time for swapping opinions. Though such a pastime is rewarding and good in its own place, opinions have never set people free. And speak simply, trusting Truth to be strong. When all is done, do you want your sister to remember the promises and personality of the Lord...or your own glorious skills of reasoning and argumentation? Hide behind the Sword.

Trust that you have made a difference, and thank your God for letting you carry His Word to your dear sister. If she takes offense at the conversation, do not rise up in confrontation (yet -- later you will learn to challenge her). Just encourage her to seek the Lord. More likely she will thank you for the revitalizing reminder. Invite her to join you in thanking God! Smile in praise and take a step back while she contemplates the Truth that sets her free.

Sincerely,
‹you look for the signature, but are blinded by a beautiful sunset›

PROTECT -- LESSON 12. FREEDOM OF THE SPIRIT

"Let the peace of Christ rule in your hearts, since as members of one body you were called to peace. And be thankful."
-- Colossians 3:15

"For you did not receive a spirit that makes you a slave again to fear, but you received the Spirit of sonship. And by him we cry, "Abba, Father." The Spirit himself testifies with our spirit that we are God's children. Now if we are children, then we are heirs—heirs of God and co-heirs with Christ, if indeed we share in his sufferings in order that we may also share in his glory."
-- Romans 8:15-17

"Look! I see four men walking around in the fire, unbound and unharmed, and the fourth looks like a son of the gods."
-- King Nebuchadnezzar (Daniel 3:25)

Assassination is such an elegant solution, depending on the problem. Not necessarily the best employment for a Shadow Gentleman, who cares more for eternal righteousness than short-term elegance -- but there is a charming simplicity in striking the root of the problem.

Of course we are more subtle than assassins. We know the root of any problem does not lie in the life of a single tyrant, but deep in his heart, in his spirit -- and in the spirits of all of mankind, for humans are spiritual creatures.

When Christ died, He got to the heart of the matter. Instead of dealing with mere symptoms, He crushed the serpent's head. The suffering in this world is only the death throes of sin -- and soon, as is written in Romans, those who belong to Christ will be done with the suffering. "Yet what we suffer now is nothing compared to the glory he will reveal to us later. For all creation is waiting eagerly for that future day when God will reveal who his children really are." (Romans 8:18-19)

But we are not alone in the meantime! The Spirit is not only a promise, but a present power.

> *"God has not given us the spirit of fear, but the spirit of power, of courage and resolution, to meet difficulties and dangers; the spirit of love to him, which will carry us through opposition. And the spirit of a sound mind, quietness of mind. The Holy Spirit is not the author of a timid or cowardly disposition, or of slavish fears. We are likely to bear afflictions well, when we have strength and power from God to enable us to bear them."*
> *-- Matthew Henry's Concise Commentary on the Bible, 2 Timothy 1*

And this is what freedom of the Spirit means, here, for us -- we can walk joyously with God through the fire, unbound and unharmed. Our hope is in Heaven even while our feet are on the Earth. We have already started living a new life. A thousand challenges and temptations rise up, but "in all these things we are more than conquerors through Him who loved us." (Romans 8:37)

All of this is easy, yes? Obviously our sister should walk humbly with her God, enjoying His love and friendship and the freedom to obey Him. Obviously she should be filled up with new life and never need to be afraid again. Spiritual freedom is marvelous, uplifting and best of all, real.

But I have another question for you. I do not like to ask it. I do not want to ask it. It is not easy or fun to think about, because it threatens our sisters' strength and freedom. Do you believe there is such a thing as Evil: angry, dark, destructive, real and powerful?

PROTECT -- LESSON 13. OUR ENEMY

"There are two equal and opposite errors into which our race can fall about the devils. One is to disbelieve in their existence. The other is to believe, and to feel an excessive and unhealthy interest in them."
-- C.S. Lewis (Preface to The Screwtape Letters)

"Be self-controlled and alert. Your enemy the devil prowls around like a roaring lion looking for someone to devour."
-- 1 Peter 5:8

Spiritual freedom, I have said, is the heart of the matter. So too, the spiritual battlefield is the heart of the war. Some of you do not believe in demons. You are above such superstitions.

Jesus Christ was not above such superstitions. He demonstrated power over evil spirits (Mark 1:25-27 is one of many examples). He also gave His disciples authority to drive out evil spirits. (Matthew 10:1) Do you doubt the existence of Satan? The Son of God saw him fall like lightning from Heaven. (Luke 10:18) Was He just imagining things?

You cannot defend your sisters against a threat which you do not believe exists! As a Christian and as a brother-in-Christ you must take God seriously when He says (through His servant Paul) that our struggle "is not against flesh and blood, but against the rulers, against the authorities, against the powers of this dark world and against the spiritual forces of evil in the heavenly realms." (Ephesians 6:12)

These are our real enemies! The confused people, the evil people, the sinners and liars of this world are not our enemies -- they are prisoners of war, taken captive by the devil to do his will. Guilty, yes, as we were once guilty. Hopelessly trapped as we were once trapped. We should deal gently with such people, in the hope that they will turn to God and be set free. (2 Timothy 2:24-26)

The devil and his demons...these are the powers of darkness. But darkness is surprisingly prettified in our world. "Satan himself masquerades as an angel of light. It is not surprising, then, if his servants masquerade as servants of righteousness." (2 Corinthians 11:14-15) So do not scoff at the idea of a man in red tights, flaming horns, fu manchu, pitchfork at the ready. Demons are good at looking and sounding innocent and beautiful, promising prosperity and hope and happiness, even (self-)righteousness. The devil is intelligent. He will devour whoever he can, however he can.

Why? Because he is at war with the Lord. He would keep everyone spiritually enslaved, separated forever from God's love. He is too late to kill your sister, praise God! Now that she has been saved, she is safe with Christ forever.

Nothing, not even demons, can snatch her out of the Father's hand, own her, or take away her eternal life. (Romans 8:38, John 10:28) But demons can and will lie to her, tempt her, try to convince her to keep living like a slave instead of a free, strong and beautifully holy princess of Heaven. They will try to scare her, though God has not given her a spirit of fear. (Romans 8:15, 2 Timothy 1:7)

These are the unseen enemies we fight against every day as Shadow Gentlemen and sons of God. These are the true rulers of the world. But thank God! They will not rule forever. The Mighty One will judge them in the end, and they will get what they deserve. (1 Corinthians 11:15)

PROTECT -- LESSON 14. VICTORY IN JESUS

"Then Christian began to be afraid, and to wonder whether to go back or to stand his ground. But he remembered that he had no armor for his back, and therefore thought that to turn around might give Apollyon greater ease to pierce him with darts; therefore he resolved to venture and stand his ground."
-- Pilgrim's Progress, by John Bunyan

So the world is ruled by forces of spiritual darkness. How disappointing.

Happily we are not powerless against them. In fact quite the opposite, as long as we stay close to God. Remember that Satan has already been defeated, but also that "he is filled with fury, because he knows that his time is short." (Revelation 12:12) The war is decided, but the battle rages a while longer, and as brothers we ought to be vigilant.

In this chapter I would like to provide you with assurance of our victory in the Lord. Then you will put on your spiritual armor, and I pray that you will awaken to your surroundings.

"I saw Satan fall like lightning from Heaven," says Jesus to His disciples. Not a victorious swoop, but a defeated tumble, for next He says, "I have given you authority to trample on snakes and scorpions and to overcome all the power of the enemy; nothing will harm you." (Luke 10:18-19)

Yeah! Demon-stompin' superpowers! Just what I always wanted.

"However, do not rejoice that the spirits submit to you," says Jesus, "but rejoice that your names are written in Heaven." (Luke 10:20) A much better prize. Yearn for peace -- yearn for Home. And thank God He has given you demon-stompin' superpowers to clear the road!

Colossians 2:13-15, 20 explains our victory thusly:

> *"You were dead because of your sins and because your sinful nature was not yet cut away. Then God made you alive with Christ, for he forgave all our sins. He canceled the record of the charges against us and took it away by nailing it to the cross. In this way, **he disarmed the spiritual rulers and authorities**. He shamed them publicly by his victory over them on the cross....You have died with Christ, and he has set you free from the spiritual powers of this world."*

Evil spirits had authority over the old man, but the old man is crucified now! A new man has risen in every believer, alive with Christ, over whom evil spirits have no authority. In this way, God has disarmed the spiritual rulers of this world, even put them to shame...

...but let's not get cocky. After all, "even the archangel Michael, when he was disputing with the devil about the body of Moses, did not dare to bring a slanderous accusation against him, but said, 'The Lord rebuke you!'" (Jude 1:9) Rule of thumb: if the ancient captain of Heaven's armies leaves a certain battle up to his Lord, you may wish to consider not picking that particular fight either. If you are truly invincible, you need not often fight to prove it.

The Bible says we are a different kind of soldier, "for though we walk in the flesh, we are not waging war according to the flesh. For the weapons of our warfare are not of the flesh but have divine power to destroy strongholds. We destroy arguments and every lofty opinion raised against the knowledge of God, and take every thought captive to obey Christ." (2 Corinthians 10:4-5)

SKILLS REQUIRED
> Being-A-Spiritual-Ninja Skills: Armed To The Teeth
> Being-Nice-To-Girls-Skills: Squire

Sir,

You are to be light-hearted and heavily-armed, singing songs of victory above the ringing and clanking of your impenetrable defenses...but of course, this armor is invisible, silent, and weightless, because it is Spirit armor. How very appropriate for one such as you.

"Therefore put on the full armor of God, so that when the day of evil comes, you may be able to stand your ground, and after you have done everything, to stand.

Stand firm then, with the Belt of Truth buckled around your waist, with the Breastplate of Righteousness in place, and with your feet fitted with the Readiness that comes from the Gospel of Peace. In addition to all this, take up the Shield of Faith, with which you can extinguish all the flaming arrows of the evil one. Take the Helmet of Salvation and the Sword of the Spirit, which is the Word of God. And PRAY IN THE SPIRIT on all occasions with all kinds of prayers and requests. With this in mind, be alert and always keep on praying for all the saints.

Pray for me also, that whenever I open my mouth, words may be given to me so that I will fearlessly make known the mystery of the gospel....Pray that I may declare it fearlessly, as I should." (Ephesians 6:13-20)

Now we have spoken (and will speak) of Truth and Righteousness and Readiness, Peace and Faith and Salvation -- many times in this book. And such things are spoken of many times in other books. Your immediate mission is not to know more about them, but rather to Put. Them. On. These are the defenses and weapons that God has provided. Would you charge at the enemy in your pajamas? Or swap out God's inventory for your own experimental methods? Get some armor on! Stake your life on the claim that God's Armor will hold up against anything and everything the enemy can throw at you.

That's only half of it. The other half is helping to equip your sister -- which the Leadership section of this book covers more extensively. For now, as you put your armor on, just remember that you may also be called upon to be your sister's squire and help her Suit Up too. But your goal for this mission is to make yourself ready. The steps are simple:

1. Read Ephesians chapter 6.
2. Do what it says.

Sincerely,
      ‹you stare into the empty face of a sgnature without i's›

P.S. Another mission will arrive on the heels of this one. Once you are armed, do not delay!

SKILLS REQUIRED

> No skills. Only faith in Jesus, who said, incidentally, "This kind [of unclean spirit] cannot come out by anything but prayer." (Mark 9:29)

Sir,

Many promising pupils choke at this point in their training, because seeing is so often believing. But even if you do not generally see demons, you can see their work in the world, so I am going to request that you pray for your sister's spiritual protection in very specific words...not that I will specify the words. I simply care that they be specific.

That is to say, you ought not pray only, "Lord please protect my sister!" but "Lord please protect my sister from the attacks of Satan and his demons!" You must be willing to sound (to some) like a fanatic for your sisters' sake.

Whether you pray with her or alone with God, pray out loud. Is there additional power in speaking? I am inclined to say not. We have no such power in our vocal chords or anywhere else in our bodies -- but there is power in faith, and praying out loud is a test of faith. You believe, but are you willing to expose those beliefs to open air? It helps to keep you honest.

And yet...some do hold that there is power in speaking -- indeed, in speaking certain words in certain tones. And maybe you are one of these who believe that a demon cannot be bound except by the word "bind", or cannot be cast out with a simple, "Go away." But there is no Scriptural basis for believing in a particular set of Words To Use Against Demons...except for two words -- "Jesus Christ". His name is powerful, precious, and identifies us as His lil' siblings.

Therefore when you pray for God to shield your sister from dark forces, do not slip into the mindset that your words must be hyper-spiritual, hyper-inspiring, or chosen carefully from a list of approved phrases. Tell your Father about the things that you want. Acknowledge, as Jesus did, the existence of evil spirits and our need to be protected by God.

Speak, as clearly and honestly and simply as you can, your request for your sister's spiritual safety.

Pray as surely as a lamb bleating, for what lamb doubts the reality and threat and existence of wolves?

Pray as meekly as a lamb bleating, for a lamb does not talk big about anyone but his Shepherd.

Pray as specifically as possible so that later, you can praise God as specifically as possible! If you have reason to suspect a particular attack, pray for that -- but even if today is quiet, be a Praying Man.

Sincerely,
    ~the signature shuffles by undetected, disguised as a tilde~

PROTECT -- LESSON 15. ONWARD, CHRISTIAN SOLDIERS

"This soup, for one. I made it, stirred it, smelled it, not understanding.
But then I tasted it. Mm...no, I can not explain anything. Just taste it."
-- Peytr Almonet

The most important thing about your prayers is to pray them. We will not much trouble the devil if we think he is a fairy tale -- or if we think he is a pushover. Jesus knew that working against Satan is like robbing a strong man's house. You do not just brush past him and steal away his treasures without a fight! He had better be tied up before you take his stuff. (Mark 3:27)

In other words, do not take the strong man lightly. If you intend to steal back what he has stolen -- the spiritual strength of your sisters -- be prepared for a ferocious onslaught. There is only One who can tie him up, so be prepared to pray!

I do not know very much. I only know that Jesus tied up the strong man and stole me back out of the house of Satan -- and I am forever grateful, with all my heart. There are no more assignments of protection here, nothing more that I can explain. Just taste it. Keep praying and commit yourself to protecting your sisters' spirits from harm.

The Lord might lead you into deeper darkness than I have ever seen, but only as a light-bringer. You will never be alone! All I have left are odds and ends for you to take along, and maybe they will help you on the way.

- I know that "when [the devil] lies, he speaks his native language, for he is a liar and the father of lies." (John 8:44) So every time you fight for truth, you also fight against the enemy. Freedom of the Spirit and Freedom of the Mind are very tightly linked!

- I know that angels can appear in physical forms, including human forms (refer to Genesis 18 for one such story out of many). Seeing as how demons are fallen angels (Revelation 12:9), it stands to reason they can do the same. Useful information? ::shrugs::

- I know how to tell if a spirit is evil or good. "By this you know the Spirit of God: **every spirit that confesses that Jesus Christ has come in the flesh is from God;** and every spirit that does not confess Jesus is not from God." (1 John 4:2-3) Test them all, reject the bad, listen to the good, and love each other.

- I know that Jesus is your sisters' life and freedom and salvation. He is her ultimate protector and big brother! Leading her to Him is the greatest thing you can do to keep her free and strong.

As implied by the last point, leadership is the culmination of protection...but we will talk about that later, down the road. For now it's just a few more loose threads, and then on to affirmation!

"God helps those who help those who cannot help themselves."
-- I just made that up like five seconds ago

Social justice does not fit into my three point outline (how inconvenient). It has too many forms to be easily categorized. It might be physical oppression, as in the cases of abortion, starvation, and forced prostitution. Or it might be propaganda and misinformation, affecting the mind. Still other kinds of injustice can leave your sisters feeling worthless because of their gender or their position in life.

God is not okay with this. He says that "he who oppresses the poor shows contempt for their Maker." (Proverbs 14:31) Even further, those who refuse to help the hungry, the thirsty, the strangers, the naked, the sick, the prisoners -- such selfish people have rejected Christ by rejecting the needy. (Matthew 25:45)

So be a service ninja, right? Help the needy. Sure! But don't stop there. Stand up against those who take advantage of defenseless people -- as some of your sisters are defenseless. God says...

> *"Defend the cause of the weak and fatherless;*
> *maintain the rights of the poor and oppressed.*
> *Rescue the weak and needy;*
> *deliver them from the hand of the wicked."*
> *-- Psalm 82:3-4*

As you are commanded, obey. What does deliverance mean? According to Job, whom God called blameless, it involves (whether figuratively or literally, I do not know) breaking some faces. Consider this excerpt from Job 29, which incidentally is one of the greatest descriptions of godly manhood you will ever find. This is Job, reflecting on his life...

> *"All who heard me praised me.*
> *All who saw me, spoke well of me.*
> *For I assisted the poor in their need*
> *and the orphans who required help.*
> *I helped those without hope,*
> *and they blessed me.*
> *And I caused the widows' hearts to sing for joy.*
> *Everything I did was honest.*
> *Righteousness covered me like a robe,*
> *and I wore justice like a turban.*
> *I served as eyes for the blind*
> *and feet for the lame.*
> *I was a father to the poor*

and assisted strangers who needed help.
I broke the jaws of godless oppressors
and plucked their victims from their teeth."
-- Job 29:11-17

I would have put the last two lines in bold, but every other line is just as rich with the strong compassion of the protector. What does it mean to work against evil? How should a Christian stand up to the wicked oppressors of his day and age? I do not know. God knows. All I know is that somehow it MUST be done. And Christians -- not governments, not coalitions, not missionaries or pastors only, but Christians of every stripe must individually show courage and compassion. We must not watch passively while the downtrodden are trodden further down.

You should fight for justice because God is just. Remember that He will judge finally, and that there will not be final justice until His judgment comes -- but in the meantime He has called you to reflect His character. Remember what we talked about. Fight for peace, not for revenge.

But fight.

Many of your sisters-in-Christ are affected by wicked oppressors of every description, and it will be good for brothers to come alongside and defend them. But there is a further consideration. Too often I see women leading movements alone. Their compassion and beautiful faith drive them to take action, while Christian men blink slowly and talk about the inevitability of an imperfect world. It does not always happen so...but too often.

Praise God for the good works of our sisters! Then rub your eyes in shame for the failure of the brotherhood. We are worse than Barak, who refused to lead Israel's armies unless Deborah went along with him. (Judges 4) We have gone a step further and asked Deborah to go without us!

Sisters and brothers should work together in the name of Christ. Brothers should protect their sisters from bullies (duh), even from grown-up bullies who use political, economic, academic, and otherwise social means of oppression. The protection may take as many forms as the oppression, but always fully dependent on the Lord.

Take personal responsibility for your own conduct. Break the jaws of godless oppressors! Pluck the victims from their teeth! This is the beginning of a sprawling, nuanced topic which I do not have the time or experience to address. But I pray that God will stir up your love for justice and mercy -- in your own life, and locally, and nationally, and universally.

As a further step, read Isaiah 58. No really, put this book down and go read it. (Come right back okay??)

Do something! I don't know what. (God knows). But do it to glorify the Lord and honor Him by helping the people He created. If you are going to do it to become a Social Justice Mogul and Beloved Hero of the People, I would rather see you sit on the couch and eat cheesy puffs while the world burns.

Pray for God's mercy and salvation for the oppressed people of the world. Pray also for their oppressors.

Two of the many injustices that directly impact your sisters:

- Human Trafficking -- "Millions toil in bondage, their work and even their bodies the property of an owner....More than 2 million children are trapped in forced prostitution." (See the International Justice Mission website, ijm.org -- and also see stopthetraffik.org).

- Abortion -- for your unborn sisters and those who are mothers-to-be. (see the National Right to Life website, nrlc.org, among others)

- For the rest of it, you must keep your eyes and ears open, and especially keep your heart open. Pray that you will grow to share God's compassion for the oppressed. Make it your business.

PROTECT -- CONCLUSION

"Direct action is not always the best way. It is a far greater victory to make another see through your eyes than to close theirs forever."
-- Kreia (Star Wars, Knights of the Old Republic II: The Sith Lords)

I can close this section with the happy thought that my sisters are a little more free and strong because you love them. Thank you, sir!

Continue to protect their bodies, minds, and spirits through prayer and courageous action. Stay in shape, think about truth, and keep the Sword of the Spirit in your hand. Act honorably, so that you yourself will never become a threat.

If you see injustice, do all you can to end it, but remember that the oppressors of this world are not your ultimate enemy, for they too are oppressed -- by their own sin and pride, and by demonic lies (which sometimes take the appearance of wholesome little truths, minor misunderstandings, or harmless cultural norms).

This is why the man who fights should fight as peaceably as possible. He should dream of seeing peace restored. Do you remember the Treaty of Versailles, and its eventual failure in preventing another world war? Well, Woodrow Wilson warned that it would take a strange kind of treaty to make lasting peace -- he called it "peace without victory" in the following sense:

> *"Victory would mean peace forced upon the loser, a victor's terms imposed upon the vanquished. It would be accepted in humiliation, under duress, at an intolerable sacrifice, and would leave a sting, a resentment, a bitter memory upon which peace would rest, not permanently but only as upon quicksand....The world can be at peace only if its life is stable, and there can be no stability where the will is in rebellion, where there is not tranquility of spirit and a sense of justice, of freedom, and of right...."*
> *-- Woodrow Wilson (Peace Without Victory,*
>   *January 22, 1917)*

I do not choose to say "peace without victory" -- but I choose to say that victory is not complete without a living, breathing peace.

We will not see total peace on Earth until the return of the Prince of Peace. But we can see peace in the hearts of men and women because Jesus has already visited us once. And so I urge you, as you break the jaws of oppressors, also to *love* the oppressors.

Imagine such a complete victory -- your sisters' enemies will see what an unusual protector you are (if they see you at all). If you let Christ rule your protectivity, the world will see someone who is invincible and gentle, humble and decisive, uncompromising and very forgiving.

The changed life of your sister, free and strong, will shine with a great Light...which Light we now have the duty and pleasure to behold.

The Touch of the Master's Hand
(by Myra Brooks Welch)

'Twas battered and scarred, and the auctioneer
thought it scarcely worth his while
To waste much time on the old violin,
But held it up with a smile.
"What am I bidden, good folks," he cried,
"Who'll start the bidding for me?"
"A dollar, a dollar," then, two! Only two?
"Two dollars, and who'll make it three?
"Three dollars, once; three dollars, twice;
Going for three . . ." But no,
From the room, far back, a grey-haired man
Came forward and picked up the bow;
Then, wiping the dust from the old violin,
And tightening the loose strings,
He played a melody pure and sweet
As a caroling angel sings.

The music ceased, and the auctioneer,
With a voice that was quiet and low,
Said: "What am I bid for the old violin?"
And he held it up with the bow.
"A thousand dollars, and who'll make it two?
"Two thousand! And who'll make it three?
"Three thousand, once; three thousand, twice;
And going and gone," said he.
The people cheered, but some of them cried,
"We do not quite understand
What changed its worth?" Swift came the reply:
"The touch of a master's hand."

And many a man with life out of tune,
And battered and scarred with sin,
Is auctioned cheap to the thoughtless crowd,
Much like the old violin.
A 'mess of potage,' a glass of wine;
A game - and he travels on.
He is 'going' once, and 'going' twice,
He's 'going' and almost 'gone'.
But the Master comes and the foolish crowd
Never can quite understand
The worth of a soul and the change that's wrought
By the touch of the Master's Hand.

AFFIRM -- LESSON 1. HER STORY

"the only reason to make a fuss over a bad man is because he is not good....you cannot say if a shot hit or missed, until you know what the target was."
-- Jakeb Brasee's "High Definition" (I sound so much more reputable
  in quotes)

This is the story of your sister-in-Christ...

Before the creation of the world, God invented her and thought she was a wonderful idea -- good enough to create, good enough to die for and adopt.

He designed her perfectly, saw everything that she would become, and decided to make her. So He drew up the blueprints and said "This is what she is."

Then at the right time, He went to work, knitting her together and creating a brand new person -- fearfully, wonderfully unique. Able to praise Him like no other.

But His work was ruined immediately, not by any mistake of His, but because your sister's sinful parents were involved in her creation. She inherited their wicked ways. Sin took hold right away and broke God's beautiful work.

Or had it? He still had the blueprints -- and if you look at them closely you'll see that the original design *included* a great rescue mission! The cross of Christ was in God's mind all along. He knew this would happen when He made your sister. He knew that she would become something even greater than a perfect creature. She was to be a *redeemed* creature.

And so she was redeemed, as God intended. She freely trusted in Jesus Christ, who forgave her and saved her. The Father accepted her. The Spirit moved in and started transforming her.

She is no longer who she once was -- no longer a spiritual rebel, no longer an enemy of God. She is not a slave to sin. She is no longer hopelessly depraved. She is an unfinished work, but she is absolutely lovely. She is God's masterpiece, and He can always point to her as an example of His great mercy and generous lovingkindness.

Those blueprints define her, now. God sees what she is going to be -- the masterpiece is complete in His mind's eye. He looks at her through the lens of Jesus Christ and sees her as pure and spotless, white as snow. Darkness is not part of her definition, it is only the thing that obscures her definition.

So if you want to know, "My sister, who is she, really?"...then go back to those blueprints. Ask God for a glimpse of them. Maybe He will let you see them too, let you understand what a dazzling, precious and astounding thing He did on the day He made her. Maybe you will see a vision of the finished product, in all her righteousness and purity of spirit. At the very least, you will see that she is becoming such.

And so I plead with you, as I would plead with our sister herself -- study her story and learn it very well. Every time you think of her, know that she is God's daughter, the product of His creativity and power and wonderful love. Know that she is made in His image and reflects His glory and houses His Spirit.

When you really know her story, and when you are able to tell it back to her by the way you love her -- well then, you are affirmative.

AFFIRM -- LESSON 2. SELF-ESTEEM IS FOR LOSERS

"For God is greater than our hearts, and he knows everything."
-- 1 John 3:20

"As for me, it matters very little how I might be evaluated by you or by any human authority. I don't even trust my own judgment on this point. My conscience is clear, but that doesn't prove I'm right. It is the Lord himself who will examine me and decide."
-- 1 Corinthians 4:3-4

On a daily basis, I see people settling for high self-esteem. It makes me sick and super sad! Self-esteem is a very popular cure for unhappiness these days, but it is the milk-and-water version of real confidence.

Real confidence comes, as the Bible says, from knowing that you are forgiven by God, from knowing that He values you as His child, from knowing that you are accepted and perfectly loved by Him. To a lesser extent, it comes from being forgiven and valued and accepted and loved by other humans.

This desperate bootstrapping effort to flatter oneself...it is not confidence, it is madness. "Just believe in yourself!" is a fine sentiment as long as you are not believing something ludicrous. A liar who believes his own lies ought not to be self-satisfied. A miser who generously gives to himself ought not to be at peace. But the focus of our days is on feeling good, not on being good. It is a cotton candy castle.

Self-hatred is a sin because it denies the goodness of God's creation and redemption of oneself. But the very word "self-esteem" shows that it is obviously not the answer to self-hatred, for self-esteem is still dependent on the self -- the same self that hates. If the self is unfavorable toward itself, the worshipers of happiness say that this is a sin against their god -- why? Because low esteem is inaccurate or untrue? No, rather because it will make oneself unhappy. For them it is not a matter of discovering truth, but of creating truth -- as if proclaiming our own loveliness loudly enough will make us lovely. So instead of seeking to discover the true value of a person, they claim that nothing is detestable and that everything is excellent, even that which is really detestable.

If everything is already perfect, there is no hope of someday becoming perfect. The worshipers of happiness say to the sinner, "There is nothing at all wrong with you! Since you cannot be improved, you may as well be satisfied as you are." And so they offer contentment not through the preaching of hope, but through hopelessness. They seek to console prisoners by denying the existence of the prison. If there is no prison, you cannot escape.

Standing over against self-esteem is another school of thought known as "self-help", which is at least sensible enough to recognize room for improvement. But the ridiculous conclusion of the self-helpers is that the corrupted self which got into this mess in the first place, is the best hope for getting out of it -- and they think that somehow in the act of escaping, the self will become something different than it was. As if the simple experience of badness will endow a person with the willpower to be very good. They cry for help to the helpless self (which has already shown itself to be helpless by falling continually into wickedness).

Those who are ensnared by this philosophy believe that their value as a person depends on their own success in living up to standards (of morality, or wealth, or reputation, or peace and quiet, or your god of choice) -- in other words, that the value of the self is to be measured by its "helpfulness" towards meeting these goals.

In self-esteem and self-help there is a common thread of self-ishness. I wonder if they know there is a real world outside of the self? They seem to be chiefly concerned with illusion, with seeing what you want to see and being what you want to be. But you and I, brothers, are concerned with seeing what IS, and knowing what we ARE, and becoming what we OUGHT to be.

They expect the self to produce what is good in their eyes (either happy feelings or helpful habits). But "every good thing given and every perfect gift is from above, coming down from the Father of lights," (James 1:17) and it is in knowing Him that we discover what we really are. Instead of proclaiming our own loveliness, we ought to love Him. In time, we will come to understand that His love has made us lovely, too.

I yearn for our sister to know true confidence -- to depend on the esteem of God Himself, to judge herself by His suggested retail price, not by her own fickle feelings. I have said and will say again, your sister is worth the very death of God. That is what He paid for her: the bleeding, suffocating sacrifice of the Son, the heaping of rotten sin on His pristine soul. And because of His love, she was worth it.

She needs brothers that know this and attest to it...good brothers to counteract the effect of evil men, and more than that, to help her live inside the Lord's love.

So we will be talking about affirmation, which is simply this: faithfully assuring your sister of her worthiness and beauty in God's eyes. Treating her like something precious because she is precious to her Heavenly Father. Praising what is praiseworthy in her. Thanking God for the work He is doing within her.

Affirmation literally means saying "Yes!" -- in this case, echoing God's yes. Holding forth the truth about what makes your sister valuable, and helping her to remember that she is precious even when she is condemned as worthless by spiritual doubts or cultural lies. We do this with actions, and with words, and of course with prayer. As before, our method of operation will be to focus on what is wonderful (her true value) and only pay attention to the darkness (the doubts and the lies) when it stands directly between our sister and her One True Love.

You will be pleased to hear that affirmation, more than any of our other duties, requires a marvelous degree of stealth and discretion. It is where the Shadow Gentleman has the greatest advantage over the ordinary Gentleman (and indeed it is what set me down the path).

The greatest difficulty, of course, is in the false belief that affirmation must always be a romancey thing.

AFFIRM -- LESSON 3. THE HAZARDS OF PIONEERING

"What I thought; what I said; what you heard; what you said you heard. So much room for...creativity."
-- Pearson Threepieces

We are often deceived about the real value of a person -- and for the purposes of this book, the real value of a woman. But for those men whose eyes ARE being opened, there is a jungle of misconceptions to hack through.

The deepest and greatest myth, which is evident in so many of our songs and movies and stories, is that someone cannot appreciate your true value or really understand you unless they are your "one true love". Romance and affirmation are bound up so tightly together in our minds and our culture. We are liable to think that unless someone of the opposite sex is in love with us, they cannot truly know us -- or on the other side, to think that if they truly know us, there is probably something romancey going on.

We want to affirm our sister's true value. But we want to do it without giving her the mistaken impression that we, like, *like* her.

(We will talk much later -- in an Appendix even! -- about what happens when romantic interest actually is a factor, but for now, let's think things through without that complication).

When you treat a girl like she is uniquely priceless, or when you point out something truly beautiful in her character or behavior, there is a chance she will think you are flirting. This draws attention to you, which is no good. You want to build up her understanding of herself in Christ, not increase her curiosity (or uncomfortability) about yourself!

Now please understand -- it IS brotherly to affirm your sister's value. Do not be deceived by the myth. You can really love and affirm a girl as a sister in Christ without having romantic designs. In fact, if your sister does not have brothers affirming her, she will be far more vulnerable to the attentions of any bad man who treats her like she is special! Affirming your sister in purity is a crucial part of guarding her heart. This is especially important for the single college-age crowd (my crowd) because so many girls have left the care of their father and do not yet have husbands -- so brothers are the primary male influence in their lives.

Incidentally, your sister cannot fully learn to be a lady without relating to gentlemen. First her father, then her brothers, then boyfriends/suitors, then her husband (and perhaps her sons?). None of these replaces the others (except husband replacing boyfriend/suitor, obviously) -- but tragically, brothers are sometimes nowhere to be found. That is one major reason why so many girls depend on romantic relationships for their identity as women!

So one mark of a good brother is that he treasures his sisters. One mark of a good Shadow Gentleman is that he treasures his sisters without causing them undue stress or confusion in the process. We are aiming again for *chalance*. The idea is that your sisters are so self-evidently valuable to you, that expressions of this value come easily into your words and actions. Reflexive, see? Like passing the salt. If the idea, "My sister is precious", is one of your basic premises, it will work its way into your interactions like a little bit of yeast into bread, causing the whole loaf to rise.

It should not surprise you that affirmation, like anything else, starts with prayer.

SKILLS REQUIRED
    Being-A-Nine-Year-Old-Witch Skills: First Sight, Second Thoughts

Sir,

If you intend to affirm your sisters, you had best be sure you know them. Before you tell them or show them their value, you had best be sure they are precious to you. This will not happen properly except through Christ. Because He adores them, and because you have His Spirit, you also can adore them.

In "The Wee Free Men" by Terry Pratchett, the girl Tiffany Aching is told that to find what she seeks, she must climb to the top of a high place, open her eyes...and then open them again. In the story, this is called First Sight -- it means seeing what is really there, instead of what you think is there. She is also gifted with Second Thoughts -- thoughts about the way you think. (To say nothing of Third Thoughts, which are thoughts about the way you think about the way you think).

You are not (I hope) a nine-year-old witch like Tiffany Aching, but you might consider taking a page out of her book.

So pray for a full five minutes about one of your sisters.

Pray that your eyes will be opened and opened again. When we look at someone, we often only see the person we imagine that we know...but there is so much more to be known. Ask your Father to take off your tinted goggles and show you His daughter as He sees her -- the craftsmanship He put into her body and soul, the grace she has been given, the love He has for her, the blood His Son bled for her, the beautiful work being done in her, the joy that is planned for her.

Pray for Second Thoughts, so you can see if you are thinking rightly about your sister. You should see her primarily as a redeemed, imperfect, special spiritual family member to whom you owe brotherly love. Ask God to conform your thoughts to His own.

Pray that God will show you specifically what is special about your sister (skills, virtues, experiences, spiritual gifts, physical traits). Ask Him how you can affirm your sister's general value but also her specific worthiness in these areas.

Finally, ask God to be the ultimate source of affirmation for your sister. Pray that she will find comfort, validation, encouragement and unshakable acceptance in His love. And add a P.S. to your prayer, that God will help you be a nice guy without getting caught!

Sincerely,

⟨the signature melts silently into the crowd of letters, and is gone⟩

AFFIRM -- LESSON 4. BROTHERS CAN'T BE CHOOSERS

"I solemnly command you in the presence of God and Christ Jesus and the holy angels to obey these instructions without taking sides or showing favoritism to anyone."
-- 1 Timothy 5:21

In 1 Timothy chapter 5, Paul gives Timothy a list of principles for interacting with different types of people in the church -- including our foundational principle, to treat the young women as sisters, in all purity. And then comes the verse that is written above. Show no favoritism. This is tremendously important, especially in the realm of affirmation. I might even say that it is of kind of a big deal.

As in your biological family, so in your spiritual family -- you do not choose your sisters. Girls do pay attention to how fair you treat them! Any affirmation you might have accomplished will be forfeit if you show favoritism. You cannot just love the ones you like. They are all your sisters, and you have to be a good brother to all of them. (Please note, that doesn't mean "dearest friends with all of them").

"Yes, I know, even the ugly ones," you say impatiently. And that is a good point. If you are just paying attention to the girls you find most beautiful, you have destroyed any pretense of actually being brotherly. At least you'll make the beautiful ones feel special though, right? No! When affirmation is based on looks alone, it becomes hollow and corrupt, a lie about what makes her valuable. Playing favorites even hurts the favorites. You are not really thinking of them like family -- you are just using family ties as an excuse to indulge your attractions.

But that is obvious to everyone. I am talking about more than this. You are a brother to all your sisters, not just "even the ugly ones", but even the boring ones, even the stupid ones, even the annoying ones. And your first responsibility is to kick yourself in the face, if you're so flexible, for talking that way about your sisters. Rule of thumb: if you cannot see value in the image of God, you are the one with a problem (but your eyes can be healed, thank the Lord).

Go a step further. You are a brother to all your sisters, even the beautiful ones. Even the fascinating ones, the brilliant ones, the refreshing ones. When you are consumed by romantic inclinations, or when you simply feel unworthy and unneeded by such a special person -- you are still her brother. You still have to serve, protect, affirm and lead her.

And further still. You are a brother to all your sisters, even the normal ones, the comfortable ones, the old friends and the extras, the taken-for-granteds and the never-noticeds. You have an awful lot of sisters to look after -- and looking after you. You can relax around your family, and you can take time for solitude. It's okay to have concentric circles of friends, because you don't have time to be best friends with everyone...but you can't decide not to be a brother. You can only decide to be a good brother or a bad one. Don't forget.

You are a brother to all your sisters. Nobody gets to choose their family, thank God for that!

AFFIRM -- LESSON 5. MORE THAN A PROJECT

"When you remember me, it means that you have carried something of who I am with you, that I have left some mark of who I am on who you are....For as long as you remember me, I am never entirely lost....If you forget, part of who I am will be gone."
-- Frederick Buechner

If you have been serving, then you have also been affirming whether you knew it or not. The first step in affirmation was to put your sisters' needs and comfort ahead of your own. But it cannot be the last step...

In a discussion about chivalry on <u>therebelution.org</u>, a self-proclaimed "not so fair maiden" says the following, and it is very telling.

> *"Most gentlemen that I encounter just see me as an opportunity to practice their chivalry, or maybe even to follow their call. So to speak. I think they kind of forget that I'm a person too. They almost never talk to me except to offer to do things. It's hard to accept help from someone who doesn't take any interest in me as a person and won't carry on a conversation with me"*

She goes on to say,

> *"But most gentlemen don't actually talk to me and don't know I have no real brothers and need people to be brothers to me more than I need them to hold the door. And it would probably be too much of a sacrifice for them even if they knew."*

This is what happens when we settle for expressing the "chivalrous" part of brotherly love and ignore the rest of it. You get the idea of a thickheaded, heroic knight whose goal is to rescue a woman -- any woman -- nevermind who she is, where she's been, or where his rescue might land her later. But heroism is only useful insofar as it blesses our sisters.

Chivalry is not dead, but chivalry by itself is not quite alive. It is a code, it is even a creed, but it is not a relationship. It can be used to protect and encourage relationships...or it can be used to reduce every male-female relationship down to mere gallantry and courtesy. The knightliness of a knight is no substitute for his being a man and a human and a brother.

Chivalry is a wall around a garden, or it is the maintenance of a garden. But the growing, living, breathing garden itself is something else again -- it is the friendship between a brother and sister. When you talk about nonsense together, or make cookies, or throw sticks, or praise God...that is what brings life.

A brother is someone a girl can count on, not only in the crises but also on the level ground. A brother is someone who will be not only a servant and protector (which are very important) but also a true friend and encouragement. It is a simultaneous thing. Each role makes the others convincing and effective. A brother is more than the sum of his responsibilities. (Incidentally, the Germans have a word: "gestalt". It means something so unified that it becomes more than the sum of its parts. So I recommend saying that brothers-in-Christ are *gestalt*, because that sounds awesome).

AFFIRM -- LESSON 6. FAMILY REUNION

"So now Jesus and the ones he makes holy have the same Father. That is why Jesus is not ashamed to call them his brethren"
-- Hebrews 2:11

"For whoever does the will of My Father in Heaven is My brother and sister and mother."
-- Jesus Christ (Matthew 12:50)

I have already noted that being a good brother does not always mean being a close friend (that would be impossible). This is where the idea of a spiritual family becomes very useful.

The Bible says that we are all strangers and foreigners in this world. Our true home is Heaven, and we are longing to get there. We have different customs and a different culture than the world -- or at least we ought to. That's why they look at us funny.

Imagine traveling to a different country and getting lost for a few days among people who don't speak your language. And just when you are despairing of ever seeing a familiar face again, you meet a fellow countryman! "You speak my language! Where are you from? What! Me too! Well that's wonderful, wonderful!"

It does not matter if you have never met the man before. He has more in common with you than do these others with whom you have spent the last week. He understands your origins and speaks your language.

Now imagine it turns out that he is from your home town. Remarkable! Now imagine that it turns out, he is your long lost brother whom you have never met, but you have the same parents! Ridiculous and fantastic! And imagine that you are both in this country on the same mission. The world does not seem quite so lonely anymore, does it? Even in a strange land surrounded by strangers, you are with family.

This is what the family of God should mean to your sister -- wherever she goes, among any tribe or nation, in any strange city or strange church, she should be able to find people who share her very deepest parts of life. There is relief and joy in recognizing another citizen of Heaven. "What are you doing all the way out *here*?" she might ask.

"Father sent me," you can reply, sharing a smile. Even if you are from different Earthly countries and human families, even if you speak different languages -- you have the same Spirit, the same Father, the same Savior and the same worldwide faith. You are going to the same place, and you know what it is like to be outcasts on Earth. You have the most important things in common.

Now if you found a long-lost member of your own family in the middle of the wilderness, you would greet them with a smile and a shout and offer whatever hospitality you were able. It is like a family reunion -- even if you only see a relative once or twice a year, you can instantly, comfortably slip back into the old familiar relationship. You do what you can to help them. Even if you haven't kept in touch, doesn't matter! She's family.

We all ought to aim for that same genuine happiness, that same relieved recognition at seeing a face that resembles your own. It is nice to remind each other that we are not alone. It is nice to tell each other stories of the Home that we have never seen and yet are missing so dearly -- to be for each other a breath of clean, bright air out of that far country.

AFFIRM -- LESSON 7. WHAT IS WORTH KNOWING

"Fix your thoughts on what is true, and honorable, and right, and pure, and lovely, and admirable. Think about things that are excellent and worthy of praise."
-- Philippians 4:8 (from the Bible, have you heard of it?)

If your sister is a cool breeze out of paradise then do her the honor of breathing deeply.

Now even though we all shine with God's light, we shine uniquely. I like to say that God is purest, whitest light and that all of Creation is His prism. He refracts differently through each of us. (That's what makes *individuals* so irreplaceable -- you are the only "you" we will ever get, to paraphrase Max Lucado).

Because every girl is one-of-a-kind, there can be no formula for seeking out her true beauty and goodness -- but you must seek it out after all, so that you can affirm what is really there. I can only provide general guidelines and wry commentary.

- She is saved

    - Whatever else is true of your sister, her very existence is an eternal display of God's mighty saving power. She was dead in sin, evilness, spiritual rebellion -- now she is alive again forever! As proof of God's loving sacrifice, perfect mercy and ultimate love, simply consider His daughter.

- She is blessed

    - She shines because Jesus saved her, yes, but she also shines because He *is saving* her every day. She is working out her salvation, and God is working in her. Learn her history and you will learn about God's providence and His faithful answers to prayer (maybe you will even help her recognize it too). He shows up in her every experience, to those with eyes to see.

- She is righteous

    - Although she is not yet perfect, the Spirit is transforming her. As she continues to draw her life from the life of Jesus, she will grow in love, joy, peace, patience, kindness, goodness, faithfulness, gentleness and self-control. Watch for these spiritual fruits and encourage them to flourish!

- She is gifted and talented

  o Your sister is equipped with a special set of talents and spiritual gifts. We'll need to take a closer look at these, but for now it is enough to say that she is really good at some things! Her particular proficiencies are gifts from God, and you can thank Him for making her so good at what she does. Like Father like daughter, yeah? It is His Spirit that fills her with that skill!

Well. So far you have been accustomed to gathering intelligence for a purpose. Once upon a time you spoke to your sister about her life in order to determine if there were any needs you could meet or threats you could neutralize. Now a greater challenge awaits. You must talk to your sister for no other purpose than because she is fascinating and one-of-a-kind, and because she is family. Even if you have known her for a long time, you must *meet* her anew.

THE SHADOW GENTLEMAN'S ROAD
MISSION Ten -- WELL MET

SKILLS REQUIRED
Being-A-Ninja Skills:
Disarming Affability
Being-Nice-To-Girls Skills:
Undisguise, Good Posture, Fascination

Sir,

Tremble with trepidation! Walk softly and in great anticipation. Today you will cross paths with an immortal creature, a bright and burning golem made from dust and holy breath, a piece of Heaven shipwrecked on the Earth. Today you will speak with one greater than the angels, one belonging to the Father, united with the Son, filled with the Spirit -- one designed flawlessly and destined for glory. You probably know her as Sarah or Janette or Lily, et cetera.

Your goal is to really meet your sister. Remember, the truth is that she is SO worth meeting. You want your interaction to reflect this truth. Here are some ways to communicate it gracefully:

o   SMILE when you see her (EVERY time, if your heart is in it). I know that tipping your head back and squinting is an acceptable greeting among today's gentlemen, but I have it on good sisterly authority that girls are blessed by a bit of facial animation. Show your pleasure at seeing them!

o   Realize that you are communicating with something outside of yourself. She is a sort of mystery and it is a pretty great privilege that she is talking to you (think of everything else she could be doing instead!).

o   Let your POSTURE indicate your interest. I do not mean slouching versus sitting up straight -- rather I mean facing her and looking her in the eyes. Or if you are a different type of person, then I mean humming thoughtfully and staring fixedly at a spot on the ground. Whatever you need to do to show her that you are in this moment.

o Talk to her with no agenda. Talk for the purpose of being surprised. There might be flashes of Heaven in her speech, glimpses of Christ -- pursue these lines of conversation, gratefully and not greedily. Endeavor to be guileless. Take a few minutes to understand who she is and how she came to be that person. Do not make it obvious that you are doing this on purpose. She will be able to see it well enough, and will hopefully understand the truth: that she is worth knowing.

Approach her with this sort of open mind, and you will most assuredly be blessed.

Sincerely,
‹the paper here has been dissolved by a potent acidic solution›

Tips For An Interested Life

"There is no such thing on earth as an uninteresting subject; the only thing that can exist is an uninterested person." Such are the words of G.K. Chesterton and I suggest you heed them. Cultivate as soon as you can, the *ability to be fascinated*. Expect an adventure around every corner. Get over the idea that things must have been the way they are. Considering everything else that might have happened, learn to greet each new circumstance as a wildly improbable result. Never think you have reached the end of knowing your sister. Even if you had...she is growing every day, and so you need to keep up. Maintain this attitude and you stand a good chance of being dubbed by your great-grandchildren, "spunky".

AFFIRM -- LESSON 8. BEHIND HER BACK

"I have no one else like [Timothy], who takes a genuine interest in your welfare....you know that he has proved himself."
-- Philippians 2:20, 22

Three things are vital: truth, equity, and consistency. Truth, we have just talked about -- seeing the really valuable parts of her. Equity, we also mentioned -- being a brother to your whole family, not picking and choosing.

Consistency has gotten a bit of attention (we talked a while back about how being a brother is not a part-time job but is your lifelong place in God's family). But let us think about it a little more. Now that God has begun to show you the goodness and beauty of your sister, you can begin to appreciate it out loud. Part of this is thanking your sister directly, but compliments are tricky. What say we start out under the radar?

If you only appreciated your sister to her face, I might very reasonably wonder if you were only doing it to elicit a smile and make her favorable towards you. This is called flattery, and I will thank you to leave off doing it or else break your own knees.

You need to consistently appreciate your sister even when she is not around. You need to build her up to others! Why? Because in appreciating the creation you praise the Creator. Because in affirming your sister to others, you can help them become affirmative too.

Seriously, how often do you hear people speak well of their friends in a simple side note? Probably very rarely. It comes so naturally to say things like , "Gosh, she does grate on the nerves." Not nearly so naturally to say things like, "Gee, she gives her time so willingly."

Radical honesty...I have heard people talk about radical honesty as saying whatever nasty things are on your mind. Hah. If you want to be truly radical, then say whatever *good* things are on your mind! Commend people like Paul did in most of his letters. People will look at you like you're crazy, but they will not forget the honesty of your words, or the beauty of the subject.

So long as you are careful to appreciate all of your sisters and not just one or two that you happen to fancy (because your fancies are irrelevant here, sir) -- then speaking about them behind their back will be one of the greatest ways to affirm them. Only be sure to be fair, quiet and humble, so that you will stir up thankfulness and not jealousy.

It is perfect ninja work. If you build up your sister in someone's mind, that person may start acting more kindly towards her -- something in the face or the tone will start to show more honor. It will affirm to your sister that she is indeed valuable and valued.

You will probably never be traced. Speaking words of life is like planting seeds. When the seed of respect grows to fruition in a person's heart, they may already have forgotten who planted it. And when your sister reaps the benefit, she might not consciously realize the change, and will almost certainly never ask about it. But even if word does reach her ears that you have been speaking kindly of her, and even if she comes to you to thank you for it, you can shrug happily and fade into the background saying, "I only said it because it is true."

It is easy to use a third party like that. Sneaking affirmation directly into her heart is harder. You will need to find your personal style of smuggling. I can only muse about compliments for a while and hope it helps you find your way.

AFFIRM -- LESSON 9. ON COMPLIMENTS

"I used to use false modesty to get compliments, then I found out I could use false compliments to make people insult themselves."
-- Dogbert

I am a compliment ninja, well versed in the deadly art of saying nice things. If you talk with me a while, you will not remember many pretty words, but you might feel vaguely respected. And later when pretty words would have dried up, that faint feeling might stick around or even sink in and make you feel right pretty. You will not even remember I said something, but it can change the way you think.

Anyway that is the idea, but I am not a very good ninja. Still I try, because compliments are contraband, and no border is better defended than the border between souls. Also because I like to pretend I am subtle.

Nice words have a dangerous journey to make. First they are born -- and if they are not born out of sincerity then they are already dead, for the tongue has the power of life and death, and there never was a lie with real life in. Compliments need to carry a truth, either about the value of what a person is, or the value of what a person has done. You see something good, and nice words are born.

Then they need to be spoken, and that is trouble enough. It is not always easy to point out a good thing -- why? Because appreciation is a kind of weakness, because it means admitting that a felt need was filled. Because you might give away how worried you were, how relieved you are to see something good. Or because you might be imagining it. Or because nobody will believe you, or understand you. Or because if you call something good, it will call you to be just as good. Are those reasons true? I think they can be. And maybe if all these kinds of worries are set right and your heart is ready to praise goodness, you still say nothing because you know that the compliment might never make it home.

See, after nice words are spoken, they are heard. And what is heard might not be what was said -- or not exactly. I can think of two ways a compliment gets caught. First is suspicion, that the person who said the nice thing is really just trying to get something from you. There is a sad school of thought that only believes in flattery and not in real appreciation. Second is reflection, or the idea that if a person says something nice, they must just be a nice person. If you reflect, a compliment will not change your opinion about the thing complimented, but only about the one speaking the compliment.

Suspicion is simple and I do not need to say much about it. Reflection is tricky -- it feels right sometimes. It is false humility, saying "oh surely I am not so special, but how kind of you to say." Suspicion shoots nice words down, but reflection sends them back to the sender, and it is a kind of superficial flippancy because it sees a gift without seeing what the gift means. The main reason I am a compliment ninja is because I do not want to leave a return address. Maybe if the parcel sits on the doorstep long enough, a person will break down and keep what is inside.

And that is the whole of the matter, is it not? Accepting a compliment means keeping what is inside it. It means you unpack the nice words and see what they mean, and keep the meaning with you. Granted, some nice words are empty. Some are very full. Some are spoken by people who have seen a truth and are trying so hard to put their feelings to words, so that you will have some little idea of how important is the good in you. Goodness is beautiful, and ought to be praised everywhere it shows up, praised even by clumsy tongues. Maybe especially by clumsy tongues. So you unpack the nice words and be willing to keep the truth of it, and not send it back or throw it away. You keep it, and it keeps you. And later when the pretty words have dried up, you still have the truth and it might even change you.

If you keep it, you can hold to it later on. Say someone calls you, really simply, a "good man". Will you remember? Five years from now, will it still matter? Will it sink in -- whatever you become and wherever you are, will it matter that once a long time ago, somebody really saw a good man in you? Will it become a part of who you are, or will the words just feel good for a minute in passing? Food will only nourish if you swallow. Someone gives you a gift, you keep it. Simple as that.

But we know -- we need to know -- we are not good. Not us, not by ourselves. Jesus Christ says, "Why do you call me good? Only God is good." And so He is. James says it too, "Every good thing given and every perfect gift is from above, coming down from the Father of lights." If there is any Good to be seen in this world, it comes from Him. If there is any Good to be seen in us, it is His good. We know that the glory belongs to God, and that makes us hesitant to accept a compliment (sometimes even to give a compliment). When we are at our best we do not want any glory, and accepting a compliment or a thank you feels like stealing. But I think it is not.

I think that everyone loves delivery men because they bring you nice things like pizza and flowers, and the same principle applies here. God by His generosity makes us agents of His love and goodness. Love and goodness inspire gratitude and praise. Gratitude and praise are reciprocal by definition -- they tend to go back along the same channel as whatever prompted them. We are the body of Christ, and we do not just give away His blessings to others, but we also receive their response. Where else can they respond, since we are Christ in the world? We are His ambassadors, and it is an ambassador's role to give and accept gifts on behalf of his great King. So whatever good you have to give, give it in His name, and whatever appreciation you are offered, accept it graciously and bring it back to Him. This is His pleasure, so that love may be seen from every angle, left and right, up and down, front and back. What a wonderful Lord!

SKILLS REQUIRED
    Being-A-Ninja Skills: Sly Compliments
    Being-Nice-To-Girls Skills: Untied Tongue, Radical Honesty

Sir,

The world praises the wrong things. Any woman trying to be holy and admirable and fantastic will be swimming against the spirit of the age. It makes for hard, discouraging work. She wants to be lovely -- truly beautiful. Godliness is true beauty, but how hard to believe it when nobody seems to notice!

Do you know what a difference it makes to her, when even one man does a double-take, stops and stares? Not at her bodily appearance (that's another matter) but at the beauty of her soul shining with Christ's light. In many ways, only her husband may stare deeply into the mystery of her heart. But as her brother? You can be an incredible encouragement!

Is your sister striving for godliness? Is she obeying God's commandments? Open your eyes to the true beauty of her righteousness! Cast a fiercely admiring gaze on this lovely image of God who is your sister. Smile with affectionate pride, knowing that God also smiles. But here is the very important part -- SPEAK!

What I mean is, you need to openly praise true beauty. Do not just be thankful for her modesty, THANK her for her modesty! Do not just admire her devotion, COMMEND it! Is her joy remarkable? REMARK upon it! Is she struggling to be patient? ENCOURAGE her! Reinforce the idea that her effort is worthwhile, that she is on the right path, that her virtues are really wonderful, that her holiness really is loveliness. Express this to her face and behind her back, both.

I don't mean you go around gasping in awe and spouting poetry. Subtlety and propriety! You're a brother-in-Christ who thinks his sister looks pretty, spiritually speaking. Tell her in that mindset. "Your hair looks great, sis. Also your mercy looks nice; it matches your shoes." She needs to know that men of God appreciate women of God, and her brothers are vital in communicating this message.

Sincerely,

‹the bottom of the paper has been slashed off as if by a katana, or nunchakus›

P.S. If you are having trouble sneaking encouragement and affirmation into a conversation, consider the tips on the next page.

Tips For Furtivity: Sly Compliments

- The sandwich method: offhanded, absentminded affirmation sandwiched between mundane thoughts.

  - Example: "Black licorice is my favorite! Remember the day we went to the food drive (which was awesome by the way, how you show God's compassion for the hungry -- really wonderful!) but anyway, that same day, I went home and Ma had bought this big bag of jelly beans, and I picked out all the black ones because nobody else in my family likes them..."

- The object lesson: using her virtues as an illustration of a greater point.

  - Example: "As I was saying, there is nothing 'secular' for a Christian. We can and should do *all things* to God's glory! Like the way you play softball with so much joy that it becomes a praise to the One who made you athletic, to choose one illustration out of many."

- The exclusive insult: noting something wrong with *"those people"* and making it clear that you are glad she is different. (Use sparingly. Be careful not to lapse into ugly pessimism and negativity!)

  - Example: "I think I'm spoiled by how open and honest you are. Sometimes I get fed up with all their shallow conversation! It's not like they are talking about bad things, but they never want to talk about Jesus or God's Goodness or even the deeper parts of their own lives."

- The testimonial: affirming the ways she has blessed you...that is, factually stating the *results* of her goodness instead of addressing her goodness directly. She can't disagree with a testimonial!

  - Example: "You took *SUCH* a load of stress off my mind, helping me shell all those walnuts. Good reminder that God loves me and has given me friends so I don't have to be Superman."

- The second opinion: passing along another person's thankfulness or appreciation for something she has done, you know, just FYI. (Do not steal anyone's thunder! If they are likely to talk to her again soon, leave the thanking up to them).

  - Example: "I know he would never admit it to either of us, but our old friend Henley was awfully choked up by the letter you sent. Thanks for being a good friend to him!"

Two final things. Whatever method you use, do not linger on the compliment. Speak it as a matter of course and move on with the conversation before she has time to defer it or dispute it. Move the conversation far enough along so that it would be silly for her to backtrack all the way to your incidental compliment. She will be stuck with it, huahaha.

Secondly, remember that you do not ALWAYS need to use sly compliments. Depending on her personality, your way with words, and the level of trust between you, a very direct verbal affirmation can be heartwarming and uplifting. These tips are just for the situations where it is useful to be inconspicuous.

AFFIRM -- LESSON 10. A NICHE MARKET

"What a delightful thing is the conversation of specialists! One understands absolutely nothing and it's charming."
-- Edgar Degas

Here is some surprisingly useful knowledge for affirming your sisters! Everyone has a knack for something. (My special knack is forgetting my wallet when I leave the house, but others are more useful). These knacks are given to us by God, who delights in making His children skillful and helping them use their skills creatively.

(Incidentally, if you struggle with finding your particular knacks, or if you feel like your skills are being underutilized, or if you are frustrated and restless with your life's work, please oh please oh please read "The Cure For The Common Life" by Max Lucado...the book you're holding now probably wouldn't exist if it wasn't for that one).

Hear what God's Word says about skillfulness:

> *"Look, I have specifically chosen Bezalel son of Uri, grandson of Hur, of the tribe of Judah. I have filled him with the Spirit of God, giving him great wisdom, ability, and expertise in all kinds of crafts. He is a master craftsman, expert in working with gold, silver, and bronze. He is skilled in engraving and mounting gemstones and in carving wood. He is a master at every craft!*
>
> *And I have personally appointed Oholiab son of Ahisamach, of the tribe of Dan, to be his assistant. Moreover, I have given special skill to all the gifted craftsmen so they can make all the things I have commanded you to make..."*
> *-- Exodus 31:2-6*

All the craftsmen, blessed with special skill from God! Metal workers, perfumers, tailors, potters, carpenters, tent makers, and many more. Whatever work is done, it should glorify God (there is no such thing as "worldly work" versus "sacred work", only work done in a right or wrong spirit, done well or done poorly, for right or wrong reasons).

The Bible talks a lot about each person having special work to do. I will mention one more passage, which refers to spiritual gifts instead of skill in crafts, but the principle is the same:

> *"There are different kinds of spiritual gifts, but the same Spirit is the source of them all. There are different kinds of service, but we serve the same Lord. God works in different ways, but it is the same God who does the work in all of us.*

A spiritual gift is given to each of us so we can help each other."
-- 1 Corinthians 12:4-7

It goes on to detail some particular gifts, including wise advice, special knowledge, great faith, healing, miracles, prophecy, discernment, tongues and interpretation of tongues. The Spirit of God, and He alone, distributes these gifts and decides which one each person should have.

One more bit of Biblical background and then we will take action. 1 Peter 4:10-11 says this:

> *"Each one should use whatever gift he has received to serve others, faithfully administering God's grace in its various forms. If anyone speaks, he should do it as one speaking the very words of God. If anyone serves, he should do it with the strength God provides, so that in all things God may be praised through Jesus Christ. To Him be the glory of the power for ever and ever. Amen."*

So -- that is where we stand. In the body of believers we are all small and vital components. There are things that your sister can do that nobody else could ever do, and vice versa. One of the best ways to affirm her is to highlight her gifts and talents and encourage her to use them boldly as Peter instructs.

In other words, *ask her to do things that she is good at doing.*

THE SHADOW GENTLEMAN'S ROAD
MISSION Twelve -- SEND IN THE SPECIALISTS

SKILLS REQUIRED
> Being-A-Ninja Skills: Mighty Allies
> Being-Nice-To-Girls Skills: Humble Requesting

Sir,

Even a Shadow Gentleman needs mighty allies -- and your sisters are some of the mightiest, empowered as they are by the Holy Spirit Himself. Each woman you know is irreplaceable, priceless and specially suited to completing certain missions of her own. Many pages ago, you were instructed to look for needs you were really good at meeting. Now do the opposite -- look for needs that your sister is really good at meeting, and encourage her to meet them! If purpose and duty are what your sister is missing, this will help her tremendously. (Even asking for help with "unskilled labor" can be affirmative, but here we are focusing on her specialties).

If there are needs in your own life which you think she would handle wonderfully, humbly request her assistance. Do not think to demand her service -- but remember that it is right to lean on your family members in times of trouble. It may require the choking down of arrogance before you can say "Sister, I am bad at this and you are awesome -- will you please help me?"

If you cannot think of needs in your own life, keep a sharp lookout for needs in the lives of mutual friends. In most cases, do not go to your sister on their behalf -- rather encourage them to ask her personally. This will let her know for sure that she is wanted, and as a bonus, it will cloak *you* in another layer of obscurity.

Your sister may already be very busy, or maybe she is stagnating with no one at all to serve. Either way, you can help her by sharpening her focus and helping her live in her sweet spot. When she takes an opportunity to use her special gifts and talents, she will be assured of God's special purpose for her life!

When you ask for help, tell her that you think she would be great at such-and-such and you would really appreciate her assistance. If you encourage another person to seek her help, tell them something similar -- that you know they have a difficulty, and you think so-and-so would be wonderfully useful in that regard.

Thank her sincerely, whether it is for helping you or (if you can do it without raising suspicion that you were the mastermind behind the request) for helping your mutual friend. Leave her with the warm glow of truth, knowing that she is truly useful.

Sincerely,
⟨you sense that a signature *was* here...but the trail is cold⟩

P.S. See the list on the next page for examples of how and why you might call in a sister as a specialist.

Special Skills Your Sisters May Possess, and Special Situations Which May Call For Their Application

- Good Directions

    o The navigational skills of your sisters-in-Christ will save you from doom many times over. Even if you have a GPS, ask your sisters first -- they are somewhat more in need of affirmation.

- Cake Decorator

    o Should an undecorated birthday cake ever come into your possession, ask her to decorate it. I hear the angry protests, that this is far too revolutionary, that the world is not ready for it. Rubbish, I say! Shadow Gentlemen are innovators. (Bonus points if you throw a birthday party for the sole purpose of asking her to decorate the cake).

- Bible Knowledge

    o For when you need encouragement or insight into the mind of God, and Google just won't cut it.

- Academic Genius

    o For when you (or a mutual friend) needs guidance through the Halls of Knowledge, and nobody knows them like she does.

- Fantastically Wealthy

  - Not a skill exactly -- but getting there in the first place takes a certain sort of skill. If you can help her find a legitimate opportunity to be a financial blessing, do it!

- Tying Ties

  - It is surprising how many guys do not know how to do this, and how many girls do.

- Midwife

  - I admit the skill may be rarely needed, but when it is, it *is*.

- Lumberjack (Lumberjane?)

  - As a last line of desperate defense against the Arboreal Empire.

- Musicality

  - In almost every group of friends is a musician dying to play -- at campfires, Bible studies, or for any other reasons you can devise. Guitars, certainly, but don't neglect the tamborines and triangles.

AFFIRM -- LESSON 11. TEFLON MARIONETTE

"All day long, every day, the Wemmicks did the same thing. They gave each other stickers."
-- The Wemmick Story (by Max Lucado)

Max Lucado tells the story of the Wemmicks, little wooden people who run around giving each other stickers -- golden stars for people they admire, dull gray dots for people they scorn. Punchinello was a Wemmick with so many gray dots that he was afraid to go outside! These dots were the world's lies about his value.

When we discussed protection of the mind, we skipped an entire class of lies -- lies about your sister herself, who she is and what she is worth. Basically, we skipped the dots and stars, because they require an especially delicate, Affirmative defense.

Throughout this book we have discussed your sister's true identity as a child of God and a unique, precious woman. But this is not always what she believes about herself, and it is definitely not what the world encourages her to believe. We will discuss a plan of defense in the next section, but first, familiarize yourself with some of the lies your sister resists on a daily basis. The particular content of each lie (the sub-bullet-points) might change from time to time (so keep your eyes and ears open!), but I think that the categories are pretty standard. Sin is very derivative that way. She is lied to about...

- what makes her pretty

    o "Make up your face, slim down your waist, try to look photoshopped, try to add *something* to make yourself interesting. Wear the best clothes, wear the least clothes. Everyone's looking at you -- or, nobody would ever look at you! Heap up layers of fashion and attitude...maybe they won't know you got stuck with a face and a body at birth (the humiliation!)."

- what makes her precious

    o "You are worth as much as your beauty, your politics, your popularity. Aim for a thin stomach, a fat paycheck and a cute boyfriend. Whatever you can collect and possess, whatever admirers you can scrape together on this Earth. Have some quirky friends who are a little worse off than you. Stick by your clique and stand up for your rights. That's what counts in the end."

    o "Pour yourself into a good cause. Try for an inspiring life story and a trail of grateful tears. Maybe you'll make it into Reader's Digest and be remembered well. Don't let yourself be forgotten, and don't let people know you're ad-libbing life! If you make the world a happy place, you'll have done well...don't you dare mess up and make us sad."

- what makes her womanly

  - "Flirt while you can, flaunt what you've got, and use your sexuality to your advantage. It's nothing to be ashamed of -- more like a tool at your disposal. Don't be trashy...but you get to decide what trashy means."

  - "Man, woman, no difference! Just a few minor issues of anatomy. You can do anything a man can do, and probably do it better. And what woman wouldn't want to be a slightly superior version of a man?"

- how she deserves to be treated

  - "You think you've earned the right to be loved? You'll never be loved! This world is a cold place and you've got to make your way in it without a lot of pampering from other people. What makes you so special? You'll be used unless you can learn to use people."

  - "You've worked hard and suffered enough. You deserve more than what you've got! Look at those people, better off than you even though you know you're better than them. You ought to get everything you want -- that's a woman's right! Stick up for number one and make sure everybody knows you're entitled to their very best."

- what she has to offer the world

  - "You're a speck on the edge of the universe. Nobody needs you, nobody will miss you for too long when you die, and your life won't even make a splash. You don't stand out from the crowd, but at least you're not a terrible person. Be glad to be normal."

  - "Don't stop for a minute! So much depends on you -- how could you be so selfish? How could you take time for yourself? It's our time, ours, ours! Nobody sees what you see. No one can do what you do. If you stop, it all falls down. You belong to usssssss."

Sorrowful.

All false, thank God -- but falsehoods that she is exposed to every single day. Being covered in dots is bad enough...but being covered in stars is worse, because it breeds more pride. So how can you help your sister when she is coated in stickers?

You certainly do not have the power to scrape them off. It is tempting, then, to try covering them all up with your own stickers. Never do that! You must not raise up your own regime in place of the world's tyranny. It does her no lasting good to find validation in *your* opinion either.

But...

> "One day, [Punchinello] met a Wemmick who was unlike any he'd ever met. She had no dots or stars. She was just wooden. Her name was Lucia. It wasn't that people didn't try to give her stickers; it's just that the stickers didn't stick. Some admired Lucia for having no dots, so they would run up and give her a star. But it would fall off. Some would look down on her for having no stars, so they would give her a dot. But it wouldn't stay either."

Quite a mysterious little wooden person, this Lucia. She took Punchinello to meet Eli the Carpenter -- Maker of the Wemmicks. And Eli told him the secret:

> "She has decided that what I think is more important than what anyone else thinks. The stickers only stick if you let them."

Above all our sophisticated affirmative techniques, there is only one thing that matters in the end. Your sister needs to sit and talk to and be loved by her Maker. Against a hundred thousand meaningless dots and stars, we echo the advice of stickerless Lucia: go to see Eli. He does not make mistakes.

THE SHADOW GENTLEMAN'S ROAD
MISSION Thirteen -- CHINA SHOP

SKILLS REQUIRED
      Being-A-Ninja Skills: Ambush
      Being-Nice-To-Girls Skills: Brotherly Love

Sir,

You are invisible and refreshing as a lavender breeze. But there will come a day to unfold yourself from the wind and speak in plain words. A true master of concealment knows when to reveal himself! There is no point in hiding forever.

I am not sure about the timing of this mission. Keep it close to your heart. It may help your sister endure in her greatest hour of need. Or maybe it will mean more during a tranquil season of her life, when there is no reason to do it except for brotherly love.

The mission is this: to plainly tell her that she is precious to God as His creature and daughter, and precious to you as a sister-in-Christ. You cannot honestly complete this mission unless you have chosen to have genuine brotherly love for her! The assignment is to speak that love out loud, simply and sincerely. (You should have all previous missions completed, to build up credibility).

I will be very impressed if you can do it without breaking something. Your sister's heart is like a china shop packed full of wonderfully delicate treasures -- especially the room that contains the understanding of her own beauty and worthiness. When you traipse through the china shop, you might bump some things off the shelf. You'll say the wrong thing, trouble her, and feel terrible. You'll wish you kept your distance, never got close, treated her as an acquaintance instead of a sister.

Then God will sweep up the pieces before your eyes and build a stunning mosaic, a new piece that is so very, very the essence of your sister. You will be surprised at the way He incorporates your clumsy mistakes into the work. Eventually you will realize that your sister was *designed* to have trusted, trustworthy brothers sidestepping through the shelves, afraid to touch anything but too fascinated by God's grace to keep their distance.

First things first -- make sure she knows you are speaking as a brother. Make a habit of mentioning the spiritual sibling relationship in casual conversation (that's always fun), or tell her a little about this book, or simply begin your words of affirmation with, "As your brother-in-Christ". Quite honestly, the disclaimer soon gets old...until you learn to see it as a celebration.

And then tell her the truth: Even her physical beauty springs from the spiritual beauty of a quiet and gentle spirit (1 Peter 3:4). She is precious because she is purchased with Divine blood. Her femininity encompasses her whole life, not just her sexuality; it is strong and gentle and beyond the scope of this book. She ought to be loved. She is a blessing -- a citizen of Heaven on Earth -- a joy to you and me.

Sincerely,
<your ill-advised pursuit of the signature ends inevitably in crippling via caltrops>

AFFIRM -- CONCLUSION.

Affirmation is the practice of making it *obvious* that your sister is valuable to you. It is also a form of protection against the enemy's lies about self-esteem. And like everything we do, it needs to be based on truth.

You cannot be an actor here. If your brotherly love is real, it will bless her heart. If you are only pretending because you want to be a nice guy, you will not enliven her with any amount of eloquence. That is why I have insisted that you open your eyes, and open them again! Everything that you say and do should happen because you have seen the Truth and would like to tell others about it. The Truth is not hidden from you, because you have the Spirit of God.

That raises another point. You cannot affirm your sister and condemn yourself simultaneously -- as if God valued His daughter, but not you, His son! I know I have said from the first lesson that *you are not the point* of this book or of brotherly love. But even to affirm your sisters, you yourself must look to Jesus and be affirmed. As they say...

> "When you look at yourself it should always be from the inside out....When you decide to build yourself up spiritually it helps you and others around you."
> -- Jerika Gilcreast, my sister-in-Christ

> "We're divine dirtclods. But we tend to find ourselves only focusing on the divine part or the dirtclod part. Forgetting that we are a beautiful creation has terrible implications for our self esteem and worth....On the other hand, if we forget the darkness we come from and think of ourselves more highly than we should, then we've lost what made us beautiful in the first place--the grace extended to us in the midst of our struggle."
> -- Cory Smith, my brother-in-Christ

Quite so! A few more odds and ends, now.

This is a warning that needs repeated -- she needs to find her worth in her relationship with GOD alone, not in her relationship with you. I tell my sisters truly, "If I love you, it is only because God has told me just how much HE loves you." This is important, because worshiping Family and Friends is almost as bad as worshiping Self. She should value your approval, yes -- as an expression of God's Love! Though it certainly comes with a personal touch.

This is a final suggestion for a way to be affirmative -- encourage her passions and dreams. Too few brothers do. We are wrapped up in being practical and keeping each other down-to-Earth. Well your sister is quite grown up enough to be practical or not, her choice. But she needs help (we all do!) believing that her dreams say something about the way God made her. Be the voice of adventure in a sea of Earthbound reason -- encourage her to offer her dreams to the Most Imaginative One! (For example, one of my sisters wants to open a nonprofit bakery/tea house; another wants to open a bakery/coffeehouse; and another wants to write a play...I think all of these things are feasible, delightful, and respectively delicious or dramatic, God willing).

This is a final consideration -- when you pray for open eyes, God will begin to show you how beautiful and admirable are His daughters. Whether you are single, attached or married, you may be surprised by the depth of brotherly love that you begin to experience. You might even confuse it with romantic love! All such romancey topics are discussed in Appendix A, should you happen to be looking for them.

Now we turn, eyebrows lifted, to the humbling role of godly leadership.

LEAD -- LESSON 1. POTENTIAL

"I know many things, and I know what I am not -- I am no leader. I speak with a voice that will never move others, I speak with a passion that goes unheard."
-- Kreia (Star Wars, Knights of the Old Republic II: The Sith Lords)

You have lead me to this place (yes, you, valued reader). Maybe you feel quite the opposite, that I have written the book beforehand and you have only come bumbling along so late in the day. But I tell you that I have strung my words in thousands, from the cleverest title to the dullest disclaimer, in order to find you here. I have crawled along this long bridge to fall at your statuesque feet, gasping insight into the dust.

You have brought me here by your excellent example. The truth is not open to negotiation, but as far as I can dress it, I have dressed it to please your tastes and speak to your mind. I have tried in every way to meet your impeccable expectations. Because I do not know who you are, actually, I have chosen the expedient of imagining you to be very like myself -- but only because you are such a good influence on me!

As a result, I have written a better book. Maybe it should not have mattered. Maybe I should have been able to write it even if I thought that you would not care to read it...yet I know that I could not have done so. That is precisely where leadership begins to work, where someone has failed to achieve the possible.

Now I know there are dozens of definitions of leadership. Images spring to mind: the captain charging into battle ahead of his army...the mastermind spinning conspiracies by candlelight...the tallest, loudest kid on the team...the stern, all-knowing grandmother...the longsuffering visionary pastor...the ruthless CEO...the motivational speaker...

You could get washed away in the images, and never end up blessing your sister's hearts at all. So how to practice a Shadowy, Gentle, Manly leadership? By choosing a different kind of picture!

Don't picture the leader. This is not about him. Instead, picture the people he has led...better than when he found them...brighter because of his influence...more fascinated with God...more committed to the truth...more ready to love others.

The leadership of a Shadow Gentleman is very simply then: *setting a tone of holiness and helping others become who they were born to be.* There are a thousand ways to do this in covert humility!

(I pray that in affirming her, you have already caught some glimpse of who your sister is born to be -- but if you need a reminder please refer to Affirm, Lesson One: Her Story).

In other words, we want to help our sisters, individually and as a group, to realize their potential in Christ. We are not interested in stagnation. We love our sister exactly the way she is, but we love her too much to let her stay that way. Why? Because we're nitpicky perfectionists? No! Because we know she is already on a journey.

This definition may be a little different from the first-in-line, first-to-speak, man-with-the-plan kind of leader we usually think about. Well I am here to challenge those preconceptions.

First and foremost, I challenge the idea that Leader is another word for Master, Captain, Commander. I submit a different definition.

LEAD -- LESSON 2. LEADERSHIP VERSUS AUTHORITY

"Unless he obeys, he commands."
-- The Bernard (or perhaps Barnett) Family Motto

So I tell you that brothers should lead their sisters, and you think, "Ah, he is saying that men have the authority in the family of God." But I did not say that -- nor have I denied it -- I just do not want to talk about it at all right now (though incidentally I do not believe that the role of brother-in-Christ gives you any authority or headship over your sisters).

Let us make an important distinction. We usually think that leadership and authority are the same -- but they are very different. Authority is about the right to make decisions and enforce them. It is not an inherently bad thing, but it is not leadership.

Authority by itself will never set a tone of holiness. Authority by itself will never help people become who they are born to be. It can make people act, but it cannot make them *become*. So do not think that being in an authority position is the same as being a leader. You might make many decisions, command many underlings, and achieve many goals -- but the measure of leadership is your impact upon your followers' souls.

So authority does not imply leadership. In the same way, leadership does not always imply authority! You can lead by commands, yes, but also by example, or by encouragement and challenges. You can lead by riddles and profound questions. There is a world of difference between the questions, "Who's in charge?" and "Who's your leader?"

Therefore do not lord it over your sisters. I have included leadership as a brotherly duty because it is a privilege and a responsibility for us. I have studied my sisters and discovered that they are blessed by brothers who are spiritual leaders! And so I insist that you help your sisters become who they were born to be -- not because "Daaaad put us in charge!" -- but because you love your sisters and would give anything to bless them!

But still. The world is confusing. The family of God is quite confused. Sisters hear the word "leadership" and they stiffen. They pull back, they resent it -- they think you are claiming headship, superiority, authority. They hear the word "follow" and think you are demanding blind, unthinking submission.

I thank God for giving me a few wise sisters who love to follow and who encourage me to lead, so I can learn what it really means. But the misunderstanding is still very widespread, and it has driven us gentlemen underground. While so many sisters remain scared and skeptical, we must try to help them without alarming them.

So we will focus on how to lead *without claiming authority or gaining recognition*...simply because leadership is so often seen as a means to obtain these things. We must work to undo what we have done. Before our sisters can accept the word "leadership" they must see what we mean by it. So far we have been often spineless or else domineering. We must do better than we have in the past.

You have two main tasks -- to become a trustworthy leader, and to actively lead your sisters. As always, you will aim to be taken for granted. What a joy it would be for her if good brotherly leadership became as comforting, reliable and familiar as an old sofa.

LEAD -- LESSON 3. YES AND NO

"But above all, my brothers, do not swear, either by heaven or by earth or by any other oath, but let your "yes" be yes and your "no" be no, so that you may not fall under condemnation."
-- James 5:12

Juliet:
> *"O, swear not by the moon, the inconstant moon,*
> *That monthly changes in her circled orb,*
> *Lest that thy love prove likewise variable."*

Romeo:
> *"What shall I swear by?"*

Juliet:
> *"Do not swear at all;"*

"Simply let your 'Yes' be 'Yes,' and your 'No,' 'No'; anything beyond this comes from the evil one."
-- Jesus (Matthew 5:37)

This is the first step in becoming trustworthy. The Bible says you should not have to swear by anything, but only let your "Yes" be "Yes" and your "No" be "No". In other words, mean what you say. Be true to your word. Instead of making promises, just do what you say you will do -- which is another way of saying that every single word you speak is a promise.

The Bible is right, what more can I say? Make it so. Your sister *needs* dependable brothers. She *needs* to be able to rely on you and trust you. You can be a pillar of firm reassurance to her. Not that you have to be a perfect fixer of all problems! She just needs to know that you are sincere in what you say, and that if you offer to help her, it is a real offer. She will not have to guess what you mean, and she will not have to worry about being forgotten. In this way, you will give her peace of mind.

Although it takes time to establish a reputation of dependability, you can start at once. Think of any standing agreements you have yet to fulfill, and get to fulfilling! If you get an opportunity, volunteer to take care of something for your sister, and surprise her by taking care of it in a timely fashion, without a lot of fuss. Just be forewarned that most people know, even if they do not know that they know: the fastest way to get a job done is to give it to the busiest person!

Along with being trustworthy, you should also take a first step in active leading -- immediately, if not sooner. And what is that step? Making the world a place where Jesus' name is actually spoken!

THE SHADOW GENTLEMAN'S ROAD
MISSION Fourteen -- SPEAKING OF JESUS

SKILLS REQUIRED
        Being-A-Ninja Skills: Rabbit Trails
        Being-Nice-To-Girls Skills: Worthy Words

Sir,

In a world of distractions, your sister may find it difficult to focus on what is truly good. An excellent way to lead her is to subtly turn your conversation toward God's truth and righteousness. "If you utter worthy, not worthless words," you will be God's spokesman (Jeremiah 15:19).

In preparation: pray that you yourself will become a person who is ACTUALLY FASCINATED by Jesus Christ. Pray that the God of Peace will be with your sister and help her to focus on what is worthy. Pray that she will be willing to talk about God with you even if she thinks it's weird. (Actually pray these things. Don't do this without praying, mkay? Srsly!)

Your goal: to step off the main thread of conversation and lead your sister down a rabbit trail to the contemplation of holiness. Turn a normal conversation into a Spiritual conversation. What is a Spiritual conversation? Simply a conversation that reflects the Spirit of God. The Bible says (in Malachi 3:16), "those who feared the LORD spoke with one another. The LORD paid attention and heard them, and a book of remembrance was written before him of those who feared the LORD and esteemed his name." So have a conversation that esteems the name of the LORD. You have two options.

OPTION A: Ask your sister how she is doing. Listen carefully to everything she says. When she asks how you are doing, be prepared to share a way that God has been working in your life, or something that He is teaching you. Share something that genuinely fascinates you. If you cannot think of anything, delve deep into the Bible and meet God there -- then share what you find.

OPTION B: Listen to what your sister says, and look for the presence of God in her stories. Does something that she says remind you of Jesus Christ in some way? Or of a particular Bible verse? Or does she just help you see that God really is taking care of us? Ask God to show Himself to you through your sister's stories -- and when you see Him, tell her about it.

Either way, you should aim to bring up the Lord chalantly. It is not weird to speak of your loved ones in conversation. It need not be weird to speak of Jesus Christ! Do not preach. Do not press. This is not the time for challenging your sister and hammering out doctrines. This is a time to honor the Lord in conversation. Do not use Fancy Spiritual Language. Be yourself, speak like yourself even if you think you sound...simple. Simple is not bad. Say "God is really good for protecting you"...or "It's really good to know that Jesus is coming back someday"...or "I love that porcupines exist -- God is hilariously awesome." If your sister responds eagerly, keep up the conversation. If she looks at you funny, smile and revert back to normal conversation, knowing that you have still pointed out a valuable rabbit trail.

Sincerely,
    E.P. Wudledu

LEAD -- LESSON 4. SETTING A TONE OF HOLINESS

"Imitate me, just as I also imitate Christ."
-- 1 Corinthians 11:1

"I stand for light. I stand for every honest thing. Mine is the only house to do this, and so must be especially bright."
-- Peytr Almonet

Should I share with you the greatest component of leadership? Yes. In order to be a great leader, you absolutely have got to be a great follower. You need to be following Jesus Christ with all your heart. Otherwise, where are you leading your sisters? Certainly no place worth going.

Paul was always telling people to follow his example. He also claimed to be the chief of sinners, and insisted that he had not obtained perfection -- so we know he was not suffering from delusions of grandeur. But he was not afraid to make an example of himself.

Are you so confident in the holiness of your life that you would be willing to tell your sisters, "Do as I do"? You cannot lead people to a place that you are not going.

This is not the book to tell you how to devote your entire life to Jesus Christ. (That one has already been written). But I tell you now that until you DO begin to let Jesus Christ conquer your soul, you will not bless, you will not encourage, you will not help or heal or lead your sisters. You will only mislead them. Have you forgotten? There is no middle ground.

So do it. Whatever it takes, become holy. Live so that people can follow you into the promised land, and not to their doom. They should not need to follow you for very long before they realize that they can cut out the middle man and just follow Jesus -- at which point you become a side-by-side traveling companion for eternity. Sweet.

A good example can be a wonderfully silent thing. It is a way to change the scenery. On a few occasions, I have set such a sneaky example in my own life that I did not even realize I was doing it.

I worked as a programmer for a while before finding my true calling as a starving author and ninja master. While chatting with a coworker one day, I mentioned that I was homeschooled (yea-yuh!) and he said, "I knew you were." How??? I asked him. He said it was, in large part, because I spoke of things in black and white -- very definitely, with conviction. Keep in mind, we only ever talked about programming! But I would say about some line of code, "Yyyyeah, that's a Bad Thing" or "That is Very Very Nice." I still do not understand how these phrases told him that I see the world in terms of

Glorious Good and Festering Evil. But he saw it! My cosmic philosophy shone through in the way I spoke about work, and I did not need to preach or be pretentious. I did not even need to know what I was doing. I just held tightly to absolutes, because my God is Unchangeable and Everlasting.

I have set other subtle examples (this is not to boast -- God made it possible, 'cuz I am not really that slick). For instance, after a few years of walking around college playing Tetris on my calculator, my neighbors forced me to join Campus Crusade for Christ (thanks, Katie & Kristen!). A semester and a half later, everyone else graduated. I and three others leftover were suddenly turned into leaders! A big step away from Tetris. Now before I became a leader, there had been a good deal of bickering between some members of Campus Crusade for Christ and other clubs on campus. They all were eager to continue the drama. They would often speak to me about it, either accusing me of hating people, or else encouraging me to hate people. But I have a very powerful, almost aggressive indifference to drama. I had a Good News to spread and a Bible to study. I was interested in everybody, but not at all interested in their wounded pride. Well apparently I exude a calming aura that helps people to see the stupidity of their trivial self-absorption. And I never even knew it! I looked around one day to discover that our enemies on campus had become our friends. I wonder if they even quite knew why. It was weird, but good.

I do not say that I have always set a good example. But in these instances, I would confidently tell anyone in the world to follow my example: learn to discern good from bad, and learn when to put aside a petty squabble.

The genius of such examples is that I said nothing directly. Mostly I just blinked a lot, or called things what they were. I focused on Goodness and Truth and Beauty and spent most of my words in honor of these. I spared a thought for real problems, but had little patience with complaints for complaints' sake. And considering my past example, I begin to think I have gotten lazy and ought to kick things up a notch in the present. Join me?

There are a lot of ways that a changed life speaks for itself.

Suggestions:

- Honor Christ with your words. Let your conversation be suspiciously devoid of destruction.

- Honor Christ with your schedule. Do things because they are emphatically good. Depending on the timing, it may be emphatically good to babysit, or to lead a Bible study, or to attend a party, or to stare at clouds. God knows. Ask Him.

- Honor Christ with your money. Spend it in praise! Worldly men are sad and scared about money whether they have much or little. You, be joyful and generous, prudent and humble. As Jesus said, the birds do not worry how God will feed them -- and He loves you more than birds.

- Do not be afraid. Look for ways to do what is right in any situation, instead of bemoaning the situation.

This is not a comprehensive list. But I want you to see how a changed life speaks for itself. Imagine how you could encourage your sisters simply by living like this. No boasting necessary! They will see it for themselves, and if you keep quiet, they will never know you did it on purpose. Brilliant!

Of course, it will never work if your main purpose is to set a good example. Your main purpose must be a deep longing for God and a commitment to obey Him because He is perfectly mighty, and loving, and good. This chapter is just to encourage you to keep following your First Love. Do not let a passion for leadership distract you from following Christ. Following Christ IS good leadership.

Be prepared for difficulties. A good example always calls others to be better, but they do not always appreciate the call. Some of your sisters might resent the brightness of your life. They will say the stink of it stings their nose, when really the glow of it burns their eyes. If this happens, stand firm but gentle in your obedience!

But I know that many of your sisters will respond with positive happiness to see their brother setting a tone of holiness in his words and actions. Credit God. If you are very sly, they will remember the tone long after they have forgotten who set it -- and they will magnify the Lord!

LEAD -- LESSON 5. GIVING COUNSEL

"Why do people depend on each other? In the end you're on your own. I'm fine by myself now. I have all the skills I need to survive. I'm not a child anymore...That's a lie. I don't know anything. I'm confused. I don't want to depend on anyone. How can I do that? Someone tell me...Someone? So I'll end up depending on others after all..."
-- Squall Leonhart (Final Fantasy VIII)

"Men listened to me expectantly, waiting in silence for my counsel. After I had spoken, they spoke no more; my words fell gently on their ears. They waited for me as for showers and drank in my words as the spring rain."
-- Job (Job 29:21-23)

A man of reliable word and honorable action can never remain anonymous. I know that you have been training to stay out of sight. Good, but did you think you could hide forever? Not if you have proven yourself dependable!

Our purpose, remember, is to lead without claiming authority or gaining recognition. But a trustworthy brother will eventually be trusted. And if your sister trusts you, she is probably going to ask your advice at some point, about some thing. Now we are not all appointed to be advisers, but this chapter is for those times when you find yourself suddenly in the role.

Advice must be personal and not anonymous (otherwise you end up with a creepy Phantom of the Opera thing going on...no, just no). So you cannot be totally invisible while giving advice, but you can definitely give advice without claiming authority or gaining recognition!

You might accuse me of gross oversimplification, but here is the way a Shadow Gentleman advises his sister when she asks for his input:

- he reminds her of God's Love,

- he helps her think about what God's Word says,

- he encourages her to choose God's Righteousness in any scenario,

- and he prays with her that God will give her the courage and wisdom to choose rightly.

Obviously this script leaves room for improvisation. But these are the four things you cannot leave out. I will restate them because they are that important:

- the unquenchable power of True Love,

- the eternally faithful authority of Scripture,

- the primacy of Right and Wrong in making decisions,

- and the reality that the Almighty really does answer our prayers.

They are all hugely significant. In my sphere of society, I believe that Right and Wrong are the most often cast aside. We have a lot of other "factors" that we use to decide things -- like what will make people happy, or what will be convenient, or what I have really earned or what I've got coming to me! So I have seen righteousness sadly neglected. Which of these four things (Love, Scripture, Holiness, and Prayer) is most neglected in your circle when people seek advice?

As for our staying out of the limelight...these four points are happily all about God! It is His Love that gives her hope and comfort, and calls her to love Him in return. It is His Word that teaches and transforms her, and reveals His will in a situation. It is His Holiness that always needs to be the deciding factor. And it is talking to Him and being filled with His Spirit that will really set her on the right path.

So. No recognition for you, at least not intentionally. Like we discussed a while back, the messenger usually gets some residual credit. That's fine, just be sure to bring it back to God in your time alone with Him. And when your sister asks your advice (because you have proven yourself trustworthy and Christlike, right?), do your best to turn her thoughts back to the Lord where she will find perfect peace.

After all of that is done, you may offer your own opinions -- and I believe that very often God gives us a framework of righteousness and allows us to innovate within that framework...which is just a fancy way of saying, "Do whatcha want!" as long as it is done in truth, love and faith. Please do offer your opinion if she wants it, because your opinion is unique and therefore valuable (unless it's ungodly, in which case, rubbish).

Other times (in fact, many many times), your sister will want someone to care about her problems without suggesting a solution. Remember where you are then? Back to service, affirmation, maybe even protection. Even in those cases, you can strive to set a tone of holiness through your well-placed thoughtful *hmmmmms*.

But what about when your sister would never dream of asking for advice, desperately though she needs it? Then you are walking on very adventurous ground, for you may need to take initiative and present her with...a challenge.

SKILLS REQUIRED
      Being-A-Ninja Skills: Pointed Questions
      Being-Nice-To-Girls Skills: Gentle Candor

Sir,

"My dear brothers and sisters, if someone among you wanders away from the truth and is brought back, you can be sure that whoever brings the sinner back will save that person from death and bring about the forgiveness of many sins." So says James, eponymous author of that Biblical book.

Maybe your sister has wandered. We all do sometimes. Praise God, He has given us brothers and sisters to help us examine our lives. When we have tripped into darkness, it is good to have a friend bringing light. In this mission, you will be that friend. Don't ignore your sister or leave her Alone!

Pray for yourself. Ask God to give you a love of light and truth and goodness. Ask for wisdom.

Now pray five minutes for your sister, and ask God if there is an area of her life which needs challenging. Has she wandered from the truth? If nothing occurs to you after thought and prayer, then thank God that your sisters are in a good place and are following Him faithfully!

But if you see a problem in her life, then "you who are godly should gently and humbly help that person back onto the right path." If you are not godly, tend to the plank in your own eye first. And even if your eyes are clear, "be careful not to fall into the same temptation yourself". (Galatians 6:1)

Now the challenge begins. Again you have two options, direct and indirect.

OPTION A: Speak out in love, simplicity and humility. Say "I am concerned about this area of your life. I do not think it pleases and honors God to the fullest. I think you have room for growth and opportunity for improvement!" In preparation, consider running the "Speaking of Jesus" mission for your chosen topic. Option A is good if your sister trusts you very much and appreciates frankness.

OPTION B: Ask questions that bring her to a point of decision. This way is less noticeable, more difficult and potentially more annoying -- therefore it is my favorite. It is a delicate procedure, so please find more detailed instructions attached to the end of this mission. When you believe that your sister would reject an open challenge, try to open her mind to holiness in this way. "Gently and humbly", see?

Whatever method you choose, challenge your sister lovingly to live a life worthy of the Lord. Your goal is not to make her agree with you! Your goal is for her to surrender to Christ and courageously follow His commands. She might turn out very different than you expect, but you should be thankful that the world is still full of surprises. If you would restore her -- watch and pray.

Sincerely,
<you see a faint glint of light and a human silhouette
...probably just your eyes playing tricks again>

Tips for Furtivity: Pointed Questions

Thank you for taking the time to challenge and sharpen your sister! Sometimes you will find that being blunt is not the best way to approach a situation. The next lesson deals with the WHY of gentleness, humility and patience in leadership. But in this here black box, we will simply deal with the HOW.

Taking an example, let's say that your sister is harboring unforgiveness in her heart against someone. The straightforward method of dealing with this is to say, "Guess what??? You have to forgive them! The Bible (you know that book?) says that you don't really have a choice, unless you're cool with sinning."

The funny part is that you would be absolutely right. But you probably know from personal experience that sometimes, you need more than information. You need *help*. One way to be helpful is by asking the right questions. It is a difficult skill to learn, but very useful.

Imaginary dialogue! (Notice the very concrete questions -- none of that psychoanalytic jibba jabba)

You: "Sister dearest, how has this person wronged you?"

Her: "It's not so much that they wronged me! I've forgiven them for THAT. The really unforgiveable part is that they don't even REALIZE they have hurt me."

You: "Have you told them as much?"

Her: "I try, but you know how it is, nothing gets through. They think everything is fine. Ggggh!"

You: "Understandably irritating. Can I ask what you mean by 'unforgiveable'?"

Her: "Um, it's what it sounds like -- not able to be forgiven."

You: "Mkay, so now I am interested in the theory of this! What makes cluelessness such a terrible sin compared to all others? I am genuinely interested in the answer."

Her: "Well...I guess as a sin it isn't worse than others. It is just really hard for me to forgive because it makes me feel useless and ignored!"

You: "Sis, this is very interesting. Thank you. My final thought is simply that Jesus will never ever ignore you or call you useless. Even when you're clueless. =)"

Her: "Brother, I have realized a profound truth! I have been looking to this person, and not to Jesus, for my ultimate satisfaction. And I have not treated them with the same grace that Christ has shown to me. Please forgive me, Lord! And now that I have accepted Your forgiveness, I forgive them in the same fashion. Brother, you probably do not realize it, but your bumbling and seemingly random questions have actually helped me toward this sudden and startling transformation! Also how did you speak an emoticon because that's kind of awesome?"

LEAD -- LESSON 6. DON'T GO WHERE I CAN'T FOLLOW

"All teachers...are all alike in one respect and suffer a similar and inescapable dilemma: they cannot enable any one of their students to understand the meaning of the words and the the teaching in the Bible....they cannot make us understand, at least not until we have passed through some personal experience by which illumination can come to us.

One who has been saved sees meanings in the words savior and saved, which no one else can fathom. The real meaning of broken-hearted is known only to those whose hearts have actually been broken.

So I cannot, and I do not say to you in this book, 'You must really try to see what I have seen.' But what I do say to everyone, and I say it with a heart full of joy and love and thankfulness, is this: Oh, don't you want to see much more than you have seen?"
-- Hannah Hurnard ("Winged Life")

A lengthy quote to start a chapter, but please read it carefully, because it contains the reasoning behind our methods of leadership. We do not try to lead our sister *to a conclusion*. Rather we try to lead her *through an experience*...or to the first step of an experience (trusting Christ for every step after that).

Many knowledgeable Christian brothers fail at this point. They have learned what is right and true, but they forget that they have *learned* it. Now they only know that they know it, and they expect others to know it too. No time for learning!

But that is wrong. There must be time for learning. It took you years to get where you are today. Years of God shaping you and teaching you very patiently. It is not fair or reasonable to expect your sisters to change overnight -- although overnight changes happen sometimes and they are a lovely surprise!

I encourage you towards patience, then. Try to understand what has made your sister who she is. Try to understand how she learns best, and what God is doing in her life right now. Discover how you fit into His timing!

In addition to timing, consider another tip. There is an old maxim that says a good leader never gives orders that he knows will not be followed. Now, our brand of leadership does not involve giving orders, but this saying does remind me of a quote from The Lord of the Rings (although really, what *doesn't* remind me of a quote from The Lord of the Rings?). In the movie, after being left behind by Frodo, Sam cries "Don't go where I can't follow!"

This is an absolutely wonderful principle of leadership. Don't lead where your sister can't follow!

Example: maybe your sister is worried what the world thinks of her. Maybe she hesitates to stand up for Christianity sometimes because she is afraid to be mocked. Well it might not be possible to lead her immediately into fearlessness. It would be unfair to expect her to transform without a struggle. But you can try leading her into thankfulness that God has not given her a spirit of fear! Praising Him for His provision is a wonderful place to start.

I am not a gradual man. I dislike changing things by degrees when I know they are so very, very off the mark. But I am learning to treat humans humanly, and to match myself to my sister's pace. When she is not well enough to sprint, I am learning to slowly walk or even crawl beside her. You too should learn to lead who she *is*, with an eye towards all she *can and will be*.

LEAD -- LESSON 7. FOOD OR MEDICINE?

After the last mission, you must rest and be reminded that leadership is not just a way to solve problems. In a perfect world, in Heaven for example, Christ will still be our beloved leader. Never be fooled into thinking that leadership means, "getting her to stop sinning."

There is much more to it. Remember our definition? *Setting a tone of holiness and helping her become who she was born to be.* So in addition to urging her away from sin, you should urge your sister on to greater heights of holiness, beauty and love for God. You should also urge her towards greater depths of humility and sacrifice.

Are you thinking of leadership as a medicine, just a way to get your sister back to "normal" so that she can be left alone?

Or are you thinking of leadership as a nourishing food, something to be enjoyed regularly, even in the happiest and healthiest of times?

I believe that leadership encompasses so much more than just Not Sinning. Think firstly about obvious problem areas, but the spiritual adventure does not end there! God is infinite and glorious, and always breathtaking to behold. If you can, beckon your sister onward. Point out more of His glory and enjoy your Heavenly Father together.

I believe that good spiritual leadership is food for your sister's soul, and that if her brothers provide it faithfully, they will see the difference in her shining eyes.

LEAD -- LESSON 8. A PRAYING MAN

"As I went down in the river to pray
studyin' about that good ol' way
and who shall wear the robe and crown
Good Lord, show me the way

Oh, sisters, let's go down
let's go down, come on down
Oh, sisters, let's go down
Down in the river to pray"
-- Down in the River to Pray

This may come as a shock, but at this point in your training, you have become a spiritual leader! You speak openly and worshipfully of Jesus. You are living a life worth imitating, in terms of faithfulness and holiness. By gentle questions and the occasional outright denunciation, you help your sisters focus on Jesus Christ.

(If you have not actually done these things yet because you are still reading, I quite understand -- this book is nigh unto impossible to put down, yes? But you MUST make sure you act upon what you read! Do not be like the man in James, who sees his face in a mirror, goes away and promptly forgets what he looks like).

BUT NOW it is time to discuss something very special and powerful -- the leadership of the Praying Man.

We take so many actions...it is easy to forget that the Lord is also moving.

We lead by examples and subtle directions...it is easy to forget that God's door is always open to us, because of Jesus. "Let us then approach the throne of grace with confidence." (Hebrews 4:16) If we want to lead our sister into an encounter with our Heavenly Father, it is good to remember the open door.

There is a certain element of surprise in it. After chasing glimpses of glory and puzzling out life's problems, it is wonderful to be able to pop into the throne room and say "Oh hi." Take your sister with you and you will bless her heart! Become the kind of son who naturally talks to his Father, and it will help your sisters to be such daughters.

I began to learn this lesson when a sister of mine expressed her absolute delight at seeing a brother or two who were happy to pray before meals, Bible studies, et cetera. For a long time, she had been stuck with a bunch of shy brothers who would only pray if she did it first. Not an ideal situation!

After many informal interviews and investigations, I can say for sure that being glad to pray is one of the greatest things you can do to lead your sisters. Whether it is praying together for her life, leading a group in prayer, or simply thanking God out loud for something fantastic -- become a Praying Man.

Well? The door is open!

SKILLS REQUIRED
> Being-A-Ninja Skills: Sudden Prayer
> Being-Nice-To-Girls Skills: Going First, Being Last

Sir,

In essence, this is Mission Zero with a hint of leadership. You must find a way to invite your sister into the throne room of God. Do not worry about making reservations -- everything has been arranged. She only needs the invitation.

How would you like to pray with your sister?

Do you want to ask about her day, and pray with her about a need or struggle?

Do you want to ask for prayer for yourself, giving her the opportunity to uplift you too?

Do you want to just spontaneously thank God for being such a great God, together?

Or would you rather act in a more formalized setting, and be the one to suggest prayer before a meal or a meeting?

The choice is yours, and I trust to your discernment. If you are not sure how to proceed, haha, pray about it. But whatever you do, there is one thing you must NOT do. You must NOT be satisfied with saying, "I will pray for you!"

Sometimes it is good to say "I will pray for you." But this does not make you a Praying Man. It makes you a Will Be Praying Man. So instead, make this your catchphrase: "Can I pray for you right now?"

It may catch some of your sisters off-guard -- but actually having someone sit with her and pray with her will be incredibly significant. She will not soon forget it!

Now remember that you are doing more than praying for her. You are leading HER into prayer as well. So if she is willing, invite her to talk to your Father as well. Do not simply pray. Say "Can we pray together?"...or "The floor is open -- thoughts, comments, prayers?". Whatever it takes to let her know that you're glad to listen as well as talk.

Do not think that you need to use Fancy Language. Simple is good because it helps your sister feel less pressure. And do not think that you need to pray before she does. You should be glad to pray, even eager to pray, but also eager to listen. Either way, you have led her to speak with her Father. Thank you, sir.

Sincerely,
‹everyone remembers seeing *some* sort of signature, but no detailed descriptions are forthcoming›

LEAD -- LESSON 9. ALL TOGETHER NOW

"It has become evident to me that a secret is not worth keeping unless it is interesting enough to share."
-- Keys, of Par Posly

"None of us should wander alone, you least of all. So much depends on you."
-- Boromir (Peter Jackson's "The Lord of the Rings: The Fellowship of the Ring")

Sir, you have nearly reached the end of this book, but you have scarcely begun your training. You will be in the family of God for eternity, and I expect that you will be learning for just as long.

Now there is a final role that I will ask you to fulfill. Your sisters need this, as do your brothers, as do you yourself. You need to spread the message. The brotherhood needs to hear about its duties! The sisterhood needs to know that they can be among family wherever they go. You have undoubtedly done a magnificent job of executing your missions and giving a vague impression that there is a brother afoot.

But Shadow Gentlemen should not work alone! The reasons are very practical:

- A brotherhood being nice to girls is a lot less suspicious than one guy being nice to girls. One guy loving one girl is a surefire recipe for Romancey Misunderstandings. One guy loving all his sisters is a little less suspicious, but still unusual and potentially creepy. But when there is a strong sibling love between MANY brothers and sisters, you do not have creepiness or favoritism at all. You have Family!

- A brotherhood can start breaking knees if one of its members goes rogue.

- A brotherhood can serve, protect, affirm and lead more reliably than a single brother. No matter how strong you are, you cannot be everything that all of your sisters need in a brother. And it is good for your sister to know that she has brothers in many corners, looking after her from all directions.

- It is good to gather in the name of Jesus and talk about Him together.

- It is easy to "reflect" love from one brother (do you remember reflection?). A sister can convince herself that "he is just a nice guy". But when the *entire Christian brotherhood* begins to treat her like a precious sister, well, how is she going to explain the phenomenon except to admit that she is actually precious?

And this is my fervent hope, that the Christian brotherhood and the Christian sisterhood can learn to relate to each other in sibling love. That wherever you go, you can find family. That whatever happens between us, we know that we are brothers and sisters. That we will remember we have the same Heavenly Father.

The Lord is working in this way. I have seen Him changing hearts and minds toward brotherly love. And we can (we must!) get involved in the work, but it will not be easy. So many people are governed by fear, thinking that the safest thing is for brothers and sisters to avoid scandal by avoiding each other like the plague.

So this is our final question -- how can we lead our brothers and sisters closer together in the family of God?

LEAD -- LESSON 10. COMMUNITY

"As iron sharpens iron, so one man sharpens another."
-- Proverbs 27:17

"A truly brilliant leader, is always looking for his replacement."
-- Louis Beam (The Seditionist)

How can we lead our brothers and sisters closer together in the family of God?

Firstly (wait for it) PRAY! Ask God to make it happen.

Secondly, encourage everyone you know to buy a copy of this wonderful book and to consider our attractive lineup of related merchandise and affordable propaganda.

Thirdly, use the words BROTHER and SISTER in conversation. Use them as if it were normal. "You're a good sister-in-Christ. Is anyone up for Arby's?" At first people will think that it makes you sound like a monk, but eventually they will get used to it. This makes your intentions clear, so that when girls finally do realize that you have been sneaking around being a gentleman, they will chalk it up to your wild theories.

And finally, be the kind of brother who takes initiative to create community. Which means what exactly?

One of my sisters told me a story. She said that in her social circle, there was a group of women who would invite their Christian brothers over on a regular basis, cook them a meal, and enjoy fellowship together. But the brothers, after eating, would immediately settle in front of the television to play video games while the sisters watched. I am not against video games (seein' as how I keep quoting them, you ought to know this). But I am against spending an evening with your sisters doing something that excludes them! These men missed a chance to meet their wonderful servant sisters on a personal level -- because they were more interested in blowing things up. In case you are wondering, the former is far manlier than the latter.

But that is not the worst of it. After enjoying a meal in their sisters' house, at their sisters' expense, they never made an effort to return the favor. They never offered to serve the women in any similar way. If there was going to be a family gathering at all, the women would have to suggest it!

Forgive me -- I have painted the picture too black. These brothers-in-Christ were not despicable people. They were kind, courteous, encouraging men, devoted to Jesus Christ. But when it came to drawing the family of God closer together, they were sort of just lumps.

Let us not repeat their example. Let us look out across our sphere of influence (squinting dramatically against the sunrise) and notice where people are standing isolated. Let us call them together, help them to really meet each other, help them to discover for themselves what it means to be in the family of God.

It is not nearly as complicated as it sounds.

THE SHADOW GENTLEMAN'S ROAD
MISSION Seventeen -- FAMILY GATHERING

SKILLS REQUIRED
Being-A-Ninja Skills: Invisible Education
Being-Nice-To-Girls Skills: Lonesome Radar

Sir,

If your brothers and sisters can simply meet each other as brothers and sisters, it will go a long way toward healing the rift between them. You will help them learn for themselves about being brothers and sisters -- and they will not realize it until too late! (This prevents your being dismissed as a madman).

You will need to enlist the help of the local Christian brotherhood. Together, you should do something to reach out to your sisters -- or else, take something that is already being done, and use it to emphasize the family of God.

Now I realize that you may be a terrible Event Planner, like myself. So do not think that you must pull people together and direct them in some Great Work. Administration is a good skill for a leader, but it is not the only skill.

Pray that God will show you how to help your brothers and sisters realize the truth of each others' existence. Pray that He will remove the lies that cloud their eyes: the lie that the opposite sex is just dating material, or the lie that there is no big difference between the sexes and we are all just buddies-in-Christ.

You have progressed very far from where you began. At this point I trust your God-given creativity and wisdom will prove equal to the task. Every situation is different -- how are you going to draw the family of God closer together in your local church and social network? I am saying that you must become a leader.

Suggestions are attached, in the handy black box. Use them, or think of a suitable plan for your situation, but for your sisters' sakes do *something!* And in all of this, keep an eye out for those lonesome and often-neglected people who dearly need family ties. Also keep an eye out for those people who are so popular that everyone feels justified ignoring them. Include everyone -- you don't get to pick your family, thank God for that!

When you have put your plan into motion, stand back and watch your brothers and sisters growing closer in Christ, to the glory and praise of God. Your sisters will be glad to see that they have such a great network of support, and your brothers will be immeasurably blessed through friendship with these daughters of the Lord!

Nice.

Sincerely,

Suggestions for Taking Initiative To Create Community

Here are some suggestions to get you thinking. They range from cheesy to serious, official to casual, organized to spontaneous, active to relaxing, intellectual to emotional, and so forth. But they are all designed to get brothers and sisters interacting in a way that focuses on Christ -- because when we work together as a family, we will start treating each other like a family.

- As a brotherhood, cook a meal for your sisters and tell God "thank you" before you eat it.

- Organize a Bible study if you aren't already in one.

- Volunteer someplace nifty and invite lots of brothers and sisters to come along.

- Argue about this book.

- Thrift Bowling

  - whereupon you go to a thrift store, buy the cheapest and most ridiculous possible outfit, and go bowling in it.

  - (This can be extended to roller skating, city council meetings, et cetera).

- The next time you are with friends and they begin complaining, suggest a crusade to rectify the problem.

- Create a prayer chain with dedicated participants.

- Secret Santa in May with a 3 dollar maximum.

- Host a thought-provoking-Christian-movie night

  - Watch *Amazing Grace* if you haven't seen it

- Invite friends to eat at Chick-Fil-A (it's like tithing!)

  - While eating, sneak thought-provoking questions into the conversation.

- Go geocaching (because it's awesome).

  - Stash Bibles wherever you go, and other sweet stuff to up the ante.

LEAD -- CONCLUSION.

"Men say the sun was darkened; yet I had
Thought it beat brightly, even on -- Calvary:
And He that hung upon the Torturing Tree
Heard all the crickets singing, and was glad."
-- G.K. Chesterton (A Prayer in Darkness)

Well.

We are here. I have taught you enough to send you away: Shadow Gentleman.

I pray the calling will bring you as much peace as it has brought me -- as much laughter and as much pain and as much love for our beautiful sisters. I pray that through loving them you will learn something more of Love Himself.

I pray most of all that you will be a good brother for your sisters. They need you, for as long as God chooses to keep you on this Earth. From now until forever, they are family.

Serve your sister. Protect your sister. Affirm your sister. Lead your sister.

A leader is a man who will keep going -- who looks after his sister as long as it is called "today".

Be that kind of brother. Pray for her often. See to her needs and her safety. Show her how worthwhile she is to God and to you. And attend to your own life. Remember that in order to be a great leader, you must lead her someplace great -- and to get someplace great, you must be going there yourself. Otherwise you are a MISleader. And she has had enough of those.

Put Jesus Christ first in your life. Think in terms of righteousness. Treat your sisters-in-Christ like sisters indeed. Grace them with towers of silver. Reinforce them with cedar beams. Stand up against lies (outside the Church and within!) about the relationship between the sexes. Like everything else, Christ transforms it. By the Spirit's guidance, we will learn to treat each other like brothers and sisters. Praise God the Father for bringing us into His family!

Yes, praise Him every day. Thank Him whenever you speak with your sisters, whenever you pray for them, whenever they pray for you. Thank Him whenever they do something ridiculous and break your brain and help you think a little clearer when the dust settles. Thank Him for their loveliness and gracefulness and for the wonderful help they give.

You have learned some of what it means to be a ninja, and some of what it means to be nice to girls. Now teach others! Shake the world in secret, and trip down the dark path of the Shadow Gentleman. How can you do it? How can you love them in subtle ways? What will the Lord require of you? Whatever it is, He will show you, and it will be worth it. I thank you, on behalf of my sisters, for being their brother.

Go then. Slip through the shadows and dream of the day when there will be no night...no need for lamps or sun...for the Lord God will shine on all His children. (Revelation 22:5)

Indubitably.

APPENDIX A
EXPERT CHALLENGE

APPENDIX A -- STILL HER BROTHER

"Eventually you will want to do this for all your close sisters, but for now choose just one. Do you have a crush on her? (I see your mind!) Choose another one. Disentangling brotherly love from romantic love is..."advanced". We'll talk about it in due time, be sure of that."
-- Mission Zero (do you remember it?)

The Brotherhood of Christ is a broad group. Not all its members should be Shadows -- and perhaps not all of its member should even be Gentlemen (though all should of course be gentle men).

The principles in this book apply across the board to every kind of true and goodhearted brother, so that every kind of sister can be blessed. I know the particulars have been colored by my experience, but I have tried to keep things general.

I would love to cover every specific, but I have not lived them all! I would love to read a book about what it means to be a brother-in-Christ to biological sisters, to girlfriends, fiancées, wives; to be a brother-in-Christ in different cultures (requiring different types of ninja); I would love to hear how the understanding of the family of God is everywhere redeeming the relationship between the sexes. And I hope to, someday.

In the meantime, God has wrung me through one very specific wringer so's I can share it with you. This Appendix is about one of the most difficult (tricky, frustrating, enduring, rewarding) things you will ever do as a brother -- *loving* a sister-in-Christ whom you would much rather be in love with. When you desire romance and cannot have it (because she doesn't much like you, or because you're meant for singleness, or because you're married to someone else and it would be, you know, adulterous)...in those situations, *you are still her brother*.

You must continue to be brotherly, and I will tell you how.

APPENDIX A -- HOW FIRM A FOUNDATION

"Put first things first and we get second things thrown in; put second things first & we lose both first and second things."
-- C.S. Lewis (Letters of C.S. Lewis)

When you wake up to find that you are desperately smitten with a lady, remember: Above all else, she is your spiritual sister. (And if she is NOT a Christian, then above all else she must become one! Your emotions in that case are comparatively unimportant).

The family of God is stronger than death, runs deeper than romance, and lasts longer than marriage. Marriage ends with death -- but sisterhood endures forever, because your Father will always be her Father. A husband and wife become one flesh -- but brothers and sisters in Christ are united in one Holy Spirit, sharing affection and compassion, having the same mind, the same love and the same purpose. (Philippians 2:1-2)

If this book was about building a romantic relationship to God's glory, I would start with the foundation. At the deepest level, your foundation is Jesus Christ -- the cornerstone on which your life, the universe, and everything is built.

The next level of the foundation is the Church -- the body of Christ -- the family of God. This is where your sisters live.

Next I would mention the old adage: "Every successful romance is built on a friendship." I would modify it slightly: "Every romance that magnifies the Lord is built on brotherly love." And I would charge you to never, ever mix up the order.

A Christian couple in love are still each other's brother and sister. The sibling relationship is a cornerstone, not a stepping stone (as so many Christian relationship books unfortunately treat it). If you stop being a good brother, you will utterly fail at being a good boyfriend or a good husband. Don't take out the floor to make room for the walls. Even a castle in the clouds has rules of architecture.

But this book is not about that; and this Appendix is emphatically not about that. It is about the opposite -- maintaining and rejoicing in that foundation, even when you cannot have your castle in the clouds.

You need to have faith. You need to trust that God is drawing you into a very tight family. You need to know that the foundation will survive the storm. After emotions have whirled you around and shaken you out, she will still be your sister. You will still be her brother. Put first things first. Identify yourself with everlasting names before temporary ones. You are a suitor for a season, and a brother forever.

You don't get to choose your sisters. Unrequited love does not excuse you from the duties of brotherhood. It just means you will have to find the right way to express it.

APPENDIX A -- WHAT LOVE MEANS

"Love is a commitment of the will to the true good of another person."
-- J. Budziszewski (How To Stay Christian In College)

Some would say that falling in love is not a choice. I disagree. If it is not a choice, it is not loving, any more than the digestion of food or the growth of your fingernails is loving.

A loving child must obey; a loving spouse must give their self away; a loving friend must even be ready to die. These are choices. And that is why I like Budziszewski's definition of love well enough to put it in italics.

Her "true good" is what we have focused on throughout these pages. It does not mean a trouble-free life. It means being blessed, which in turn means resembling Christ and giving Him props, enjoying the favor of God, the world He has created, and the treasures of the faith (which are nicely described in Ephesians chapter 1).

O! when I was a moody and easily-enamored lad, how many times did I turn the phrase over in my mind, "I love her!"...Well eventually I started to get suspicious about it. A thousand wistful sighs do not add up to a drop of love, and all I was doing was sitting 'round sighing.

"Jakeb, old fellow," said I, "when do you love her?"

"From morning 'til night!" I vowed.

"No, I mean -- *when* are you actually involved in loving her? When have you ever helped her?"

"I--"

"In the immortal words of Clint Black: love isn't someplace that we fall! It's something that we do! What have you done lately?"

"I--"

"If all you ever did was laze about saying, 'Ohhhhh, tennis, I play you!'...would you be a tennis player, or just a bit stupid?"

"SIR I TAKE YOUR POINT."

I have had this conversation more times that I can remember. Not that sighing wistfully is a bad thing -- and I have embraced the poignant moments of lonely longing. But it oughn't stop me from loving the girl I like so much, nor should it stop you. Whether you ever get to experience *romantic* love, you can always be involved in the breathtakingly beautiful act of plain old Christian kindness. You are her brother forever. I cannot say it better than to quote Budzisewski again (though in order to understand the full meaning of the quote you are also going to want to read a little book called "The Four Loves" by C.S. Lewis -- because *eros* is more than a physical attraction, and *charity* is a LOT more than giving stuff to poor people). Oh, right. Quote:

> *"If you love a girl who will never love you in return, seek God's grace to sublimate your erotic love for her into the spiritual love of charity. Be grateful to God that you knew her, but be willing to fall in erotic love with someone else."*
> *-- J. "Professor Theophilus" Budzisewski*
> *(<u>boundless.org</u>, "Ask Theophilus: Farewells")*

APPENDIX A -- GOING SOMEWHERE?

If your interest in a girl goes unreturned, you will probably hear advice like Budzisewski's: "Be grateful to God that you knew her."

What, are you going somewhere? Be grateful to God that you KNOW her! No matter how many butterflies are in your stomach, she's still your beautiful sister -- you still have to be a good brother. First things first, right? You need to trust that the affection between a spiritual brother and sister is strong enough to survive a difference in levels of attraction. At the end of all the drama, will you have remained loyal?

So there are two common theories about what to do when a girl says, "I'm sorry, I'm just not interested in you in that way." You might have heard either or both of these.

- THEORY 1 (MOVE ON WITH YOUR LIFE): You can't be expected to deal with a constant, painful reminder of rejection. Spending time with her would be more like stealing, and it will only hurt you both. It is wiser and more considerate to separate yourself...still be friendly, but you shouldn't be close friends!

- THEORY 2 (STAY IN THE GAME): She says that *now*, but does she really know what she wants? She might change her mind when she realizes how much you love her, what a good thing she was giving up. She's the fool for saying no! But if you really like her, you should stick around and try to be a good friend. Eventually she'll snap out of it.

Ooh, problems. Theory 1 assumes that your emotions are out of control -- not subject to the Spirit. It assumes that if you are around a girl you like, you will naturally do selfish things to grab for her affection and attention. So choose the safe path. Flee from infatuation and avoid hurting her by giving up your role as a brother. This is the favored theory of people who think friendships between the sexes are dangerous and impossible. This leads to broken friendships and leaves both parties feeling abandoned.

Theory 2 is even worse. It is first of all condescending, assuming that your sister doesn't know her own mind, that she is just confused and needs to be shown what's best. Aside from giving no weight to her own wishes, it is also deceptive. You end up pretending to be a good brother, but you have a hidden agenda. Brotherhood in Theory 2 is a stepping stone, a way to gain her trust and manipulate it. You are just trying to stay on the inside track to put in a good word for yourself. It's a manipulative, parasitic, arrogant attempt to "make her like you".

Theory 2 goes a long way towards explaining why brothers are not trusted. It is one of the very good reasons for becoming a ninja. As for Theory 1, it contributes to the idea that even true brothers won't stick around for long, and it gives the false idea that romance is more foundational than brotherly love.

There is a sneaky little lie hiding behind *both* of these, though, and it goes down to the core of what makes your sister valuable. Have you spotted it? This is the underlying lie: *the most important reason to spend time around a sister-in-Christ is to see if she could potentially be your girlfriend.*

If she rebuffs your romantic intentions and then you shut her out of your life "for everybody's sake", what does that tell her? If you keep hanging around, poking and prodding and trying to change her mind, what does that tell her?

It tells her: *I'm not important outside of a romantic relationship. I'm not worth being loved all my life except as a wife.*

I do not care about your motivations. I do not care if it's really, really hard to stick around and be generous and feel like the smallest person in the room because she does not pay you any special attention. I know how those things hurt...I just don't care. Because the pain of rejection does not hurt nearly as much as the pain she feels, knowing that she can't hope to reject your romance while keeping your love.

Nothing hurts like believing, *No guy will ever love me unless he thinks I'll kiss him some day.*

It is hard to write a page with angry fingers -- they tend to quiver so. I am angry, furious, with guys who act this way and call themselves "in love". They slander Love! I am angry with myself when I do it, too.

We are tempted toward a deep-seated results-driven motivation, where "results" means "finding someone to belong to". You will even hear a variation of Theory 1 that goes like this: not only will backing off save you some pain, but absence makes the heart grow fonder so...y'never know. Maybe she'll come around when she sees what she's really missing.

Well that's great, champ, but guess what? Even if you win the game, you're still a player.

"I couldn't serve her, protect her, affirm her, or lead her...because I *love* her!"

No, in that case, you are using her to satisfy yourself, or abandoning her when love is inconvenient. Have you forgotten who her Father is? Don't you dare claim to be brotherly when you've really got a hidden agenda. Don't you dare pretend to be sneaky so she can "accidentally" discover your wonderfulness. Don't use your friendship as a way to get in and chip away at her resolve. If you ever think about rooting up the foundation and tearing apart the family of God just because your castle in the clouds fell down, may someone break your knees before you break your sister's heart.

There's a third option. Sublimate your romantic attraction into sacrificial, Christlike love. That means surrendering a lesser thing to Jesus Christ so that it can grow into something purer, stronger, and more complete -- kind of like Pokemon. I know it hurts. Do it anyway. Do it because you honestly care about her and have decided that loving her like a sister matters MORE than being in love with her.

Never deny the pain, but recognize that pain is not a bad thing. If your sister is such a lovely creature -- if she really is God's masterpiece -- then she is worth missing. You can even hope for her heart to change. It's been known to happen. But you absolutely can not let that be your motivation for your brotherly love. Not if you want to call it Love.

She still needs you. Maybe she needs you even more after she has rejected you -- because nobody else can prove to her that brotherly love outlasts romantic disappointment. Your painful position is the very thing to show her that the family of God is stronger than pain.

You could never do it alone, of course. But you have a Spirit who knows what love is all about. Let Him fill you and give you the ability to do it -- for the sake of the girl you love, and her Father. He will help you stick around and be a brother through it all.

When you've chosen the rough and noble road, here are some practical ways to continue...

APPENDIX A -- RAISING THE FLOOR

"He is the single most motivating man you'll meet. He is so bad at what he does, you'll be too ashamed to do any worse."
-- Pearson Threepieces
  (in discussing his lifelong friend, Bombulous Ourdenstern)

If a girl's life is not full of good men, it will likely be full of bad men. This has always been one of our motivations in staying nearby. But in the realm of romantic relationships, it takes on a sharper meaning.

If you are rejected, let this be the goal of your rejection: to set a shining example of the bare minimum. Our sisters' standards should be absolutely dizzying. The bar they set should give their boyfriends vertigo. (Not in an unreasonable sense, but in the sense of asking for his very best).

If she has never had real brothers, though, her standards are likely to be very low. The first man who calls her beautiful will have already surpassed her previous experiences.

A girl with strong brothers knows what godliness looks like. She knows that she deserves to be treated like royalty, that godly men should be Christlike, and that love should be honest. Then she can hold the thought in her head, "Even though <insert your name here> is not the one for me, he is a wonderful brother and I know that I want my future husband to love me at *least* as much as this guy does!"

Not that girls with strong brothers never end up dating despicable characters -- but it's much less likely. (Or that's the theory. I am waiting for the rise of a strong brotherhood so we can verify these things statistically).

Here are some ways to raise the floor:

- Explain, like I said, that you still love her as a sister, and you know that the guy she ends up with should be at least as good a brother as you, and hopefully a whole lot better!

- Remember that you do not *deserve* a yes, and that even if she has hurt you with her rejection, she has not *wronged* you. A sister has the right to choose, not her brothers, but her suitors.

- Pray for her always. Pray for her true good.

- Continue to serve, protect, affirm, and lead her as discussed in the rest of this book! Most of your brotherly duties remain unchanged, even with this little extra complication.

- Sometimes it is indeed necessary to put some distance between yourselves...especially if she tries to get the joys of romance out of her friendship with you. If you are providing her with love that is not purely brotherly, you are only enabling her to spend time in limbo. She must be satisfied in pure singleness or else purposefully considering what comes next. Pray for wisdom to know when brotherly love DOES mean stepping back.

- If you do remain a close brother, never use your trusted position to undermine her obedience to the Lord. I was once interested in a girl who knew that God wanted her to remain single for a season...and I faced a choice. Help her to faithfully obey? Or try to stir up her feelings for me? Not wanting to be my own arch-nemesis, and wanting to please God, I chose the former.

- Finally, and this is important enough to warrant its own section, check your frequencies!

APPENDIX A -- FREQUENCIES AND FAVORITISM

Sometimes it is hard to know how close to get to a sister. You want to be available, useful and involved -- but you also want to treat her with all purity (her body, of course, but also her heart and mind and spirit).

When you are romantically attracted to your sister-in-Christ, it gets even trickier. It is easy to cross the line, but for some people the greater danger is overcompensating and treating her like a total stranger! Even with an uncertain level of intimacy, though, you can easily keep things proper by monitoring your Frequency and checking for Favoritism.

Favoritism we have already talked about. It is bad. Do not do it. If one girl has got you enchanted, it is especially important to realize that the sisters around her are special too and should be paid equal attention. (You will probably mess things up and get the ratios wrong. If you hurt anyone in this process, humbly explain your equitable intentions and pray for her understanding).

Now Frequency is a new topic, and worth considering carefully. I have it on good authority from a panel of very wise women: the harmfulness or helpfulness of deep personal interaction depends largely on how often it is repeated.

So even if you like a girl and are trying to stay brotherly, it can be good to hug her in greetings or farewells. Indeed you should be sure to hug her about as much as you hug other sisters whom you know comparably well! But do not hug her every half hour like a creeper.

This applies not only to hugs, but also to emails, phone calls, sharing Bible verses, going out to eat (preferably not alone together), telling her she's fantastic, giving her presents...things you SHOULD do as her brother, with relatively the same frequency and transparency that you do for other sisters. Do not do them more often -- that's obviously flirtatious. Do not do them less often -- that will make her feel left out instead of raising her floor.

And in all these things, continue to ensure that you are not the center of the picture. That place is reserved for the Father, the Son, and the Holy Spirit. You are somewhere off to the side, in the background, engaged in stomping on grapes or another suitably scenic task.

Of course, being a good brother is impossible. That is, impossible on your own. That is why you are only, ever a brother IN CHRIST -- apart from Him you can do nothing.

APPENDIX A -- THE SPIRITUAL GIFT OF HATS

"Gentlemen, why do we wear hats?
So we may take them off at the time proper."
-- A Responsive Reading from the Minute Book of the Brotherhood of the
Fellowship of the Silver and Cedar Society Brethren's Coalition for the
Revolution of Traditional Niceness and General Gentlemanly Camaraderie

I like hats.

Top hats are good. Fedoras, mm, pretty nice. Country Gentleman walking hats? Yes!

I have this one hat, old-school Ralph Lauren Polo -- got it for like three bucks. Kind of a tweed Sherlock Holmes looking thing, but shaped like a baseball cap with a supersized brim. His name is Claude. Best three bucks I ever spent.

I only tell you these things as part of your training. You will need to learn to relate to your sister in the proper role -- I call this wearing the right hat. And maybe everything inside of you will yearn to wear the "Winning Her Heart" hat, but you know that real love demands you wear the "Blessing Her Heart" hat.

Trust me, you will never be able to keep your hats straight. Somehow the slick silk stovepipe with the curly moustaches always ends up on the top of the heap. The tweed duck-billed Polo hat of brotherhood gets buried under waves of emotion. Am I making myself clear?

You need to ask God for help. You will never imitate Christ, here, except by letting His Spirit fill your relationships. You might pray in desperation over your unquenchable selfishness -- and miraculously wake up caring for her like a sister again. The Holy Spirit might take the brother hat and smash it down over your ears, so you couldn't get it off if you wanted to.

I call it the Spiritual Gift of Hats, but it is not an exclusive gift. Any Christian is capable of true love. If true love requires you to keep treating her like a sister, God Himself will make you able.

Absolutely the best way to see your sister clearly is to pray for her. By praying, you will start to share God's heart for her and understand His love for her. It becomes less important that she is your favorite person, and more important that she is God's deeply beloved daughter.

Never say romance is stronger than love, because that is a lie and a coward's way out. Instead, ask God to keep your hat on straight. You will find out the impossible is possible.

APPENDIX A -- ENJOYING THE CONVENIENT, DELAYING THE GOOD

This section is a sprig of critical miscellany. My whole life long I had never thought about it, until I found an article on <u>boundless.org</u> called "Biblical Dating: Just Friends", by Scott Croft. He makes the following observations about friendships between men and women:

> *"Let's assume for the sake of argument that your intimate friendship is one of those rare jewels that is devoid of the potential for hurt or confusion. There's another drawback to such friendships. They discourage marriage...*
>
> *In the past, when both sexual immorality and intimate male-female friendships were much less accepted and less common in society, men and women moved more deliberately toward marriage earlier in life. By offering a taste of the companionship and interactions that make marriage so satisfying, with none of the accompanying commitments or responsibilities entailed in marriage, intimate friendships discourage the pursuit of the grown-up, God-intended outlet for marital desires — marriage.*
>
> *I believe Scripture to teach that engaging in the types of emotional intimacy and companionship involved in close male-female friendships — outside of marriage and for their own sake — is wrong....But even if you don't accept that premise, such intimacy is still inadvisable in the sense that it delays and discourages marriage, which Scripture unambiguously calls good and right."*

Mr. Croft poses a shrewd question, which I now pose to you: are you satisfying the intermediate needs of your sisters such that they feel no particular compulsion to pursue marriage?

If the answer is yes, changes must be made. As a brother you must encourage your sister to grow, prepare for, and seek after marriage -- even if you are afraid it will not be marriage to you. It is a terrible brother who pulls her away from that blessing (even by trying to be a substitute for it).

Do not defraud her by giving the wrong kind of emotional intimacy! Your friendship should make her free, not weaken her to keep her stuck on you.

But our proper, prudent brotherly love should be incredible nonetheless -- open, personal, loyal and joyous. The article concludes with thoughts that make me smile:

> *"I Timothy 5 describes a relationship among Christian men and*

women not married to one another as that of brothers and sisters....In fact, single brothers and sisters in Christ, like the rest of Christ's body, are positively called to care for one another. Men can (and should) give women rides home rather than have them walk alone at night. Men can come over and move couches. Women can cook a meal for a group of guys in danger of developing scurvy from a near total lack of vegetables. Knock yourselves out."

Of course we know it is much more than being parking-lot bodyguards and furniture-movers. But I am ever grateful to God for showing me the truth in this article (in fact, sort of smacking me o'er the head with it).

It is a good way to make your relationships even more wholesome. What kind of brotherly support do you want *your* wife to have? Offer that kind of support to all your sisters, giving hearty encouragement to her "pursuit of the grown-up, God-intended outlet for marital desires -- marriage."

APPENDIX A -- ENTIRELY TOO WONDERFUL

"And God said:
Be very careful around Christian girls,
for you will think you are falling in love with them,
when you are actually attracted to My Spirit inside them
(and not so much to *them*).
I am what you are longing for.
Don't be fooled."
-- The Observations of Mr. Brandon Smith (a paraphrase)

A shocking thing happens when you start being a good brother.

You start noticing things about your sister-in-Christ -- beauty that you never saw before. I think this comes mostly from affirmation. You can only insist that a girl is lovely and lovable for so long before you start to realize: it is true!

If that has happened to you on this journey, I call it a mark of success. You are seeing past the surface, down to the Spirit level. In some ways, it feels like being in love. It is fresh, fascinating and entirely unique. She is made in the image of God! Hopefully she acts like her Lord Jesus Christ; hopefully she is filled with the Spirit.

You should see all these things, rejoice in them, and treasure her more for seeing her clearer! But all of your sisters-in-Christ share the same Spirit, so you may find yourself attracted to lots of them. Do not be confused, discouraged or ashamed. You are not fickle or unstable...it is just that all of these sisters are really pointing you toward your God! The longing you feel is a longing for His Holiness, which shows up in the women whom He has made holy. And the proper response is to seek the Lord, not zero in on one of the women!

So I charge you not to lose your head and heart. Embrace the attraction as a joyous family reunion! Praise God for every godly sister. When you do genuinely fall in love, it will be an even greater addition to that wholesome affection. (It sort of raises the floor for you too, yeah?) Now,

> *"there never was a man in love who did not declare that, if he*
> *strained every nerve to breaking, he was going to have his desire.*
> *And there never was a man in love who did not declare also that*
> *he ought not to have it," [because he was unworthy].*
> *-- G.K. Chesterton, Heretics*

But even when you are a man in love, you are more than that. You are a Shadow Gentleman! As a lover you can say she is entirely too wonderful, but as a brother you are bound to remember she is still your sister-in-Christ --

real love for a real person, warts and all.

This duty of yours: Service, Protection, Affirmation, Leadership...it is nothing you acquired by being worthy for the task. This is your heritage, man. You were born (again) into it.

Breinigsville, PA USA
04 October 2009
225166BV00001B/4/P